BECOMING A
STUDENT LEADER

LEADING YOURSELF AND OTHERS

BY DAN BOAL AND LEN KAGELER

THE YOUTH CARTEL

BECOMING A STUDENT LEADER

Copyright © 2018 by Dan Boal

Publisher: Mark Oestreicher
Managing Editor: Sarah Hauge
Cover Design: Adam McLane
Layout: Marilee R. Pankratz
Creative Director: John, Son of Thunder

ISBN-13: 978-1-942145-38-7
ISBN-10: 1-942145-38-1

The Youth Cartel, LLC
www.theyouthcartel.com

Email: info@theyouthcartel.com

Born in San Diego
Printed in the U.S.A.

To my children: Everett, Arayla, Betsy, Lael, and CeCe, and the next generation of leaders, who will create new and meaningful spaces where everyone belongs.

CONTENTS

INTRODUCTION

If you are reading this book then my assumption is that you are a student leader! My hope is that a pastor, adult leader, or parent handed you this book with a desire to develop your leadership style and grow in your heart a rich understanding of what it means to follow Jesus imperfectly, and influence others to do the same.

At this moment you are awesome and full of potential. The day the foundations of the earth were spoken into existence, God also created the future possibility of you. And with you come all of the good things only you can bring into this world. The whole human race is better off because you exist. Jesus himself looks at you and is proud to call you his son or daughter. God is pleased that you are in this world, exactly as you are today. He can't wait to see who you become and the beautiful impact you will have on the world.

As the Director of Alliance Youth, the national youth ministry of the Christian and Missionary Alliance, I serve 38,000 teenagers and more than 5,000 youth workers. In my years of ministry I have spent time all over the United States and other parts of the world. I am one hundred percent convinced that each of these teenagers will have a meaningful effect on the lives of the people they encounter. However, I often hear the same story. A teenager reads the Bible and sees how

God used really messed up and broken people to do amazing things but then thinks, "I know God did it for them, but he doesn't want to do it for me." Adults have these same thoughts. Time and again I have seen this line of thinking breed doubt.

Why is it hard to believe that God could use you just like he used them? Primarily, it's because young people often believe they are disqualified from receiving the awesomeness Jesus is trying to give them. They believe the lies of the evil one. *You aren't worthy. You couldn't possibly. What makes you think you deserve this? What do you think you have to offer?*

I wrote this book to help you understand that you are loved and chosen by God. This book will help you to have a better sense of your identity and to learn how to use your gifts to do awesome things for his kingdom and glory.

When you read the Bible, you'll spend time with stories of God pursuing and using broken people, and you will begin to understand that Jesus wants to pursue and use you too. Their stories are your story. There is no difference between the Old Testament prophet Elijah and you. His story starts in 1 Kings 17. Elijah performed incredible miracles. He prayed for a drought and it lasted three years. He caused fire to come down from the sky and he once raised a child from the dead. Yet, he suffered intense bouts of loneliness and possible depression. Elijah was often prideful, yet he showed a significant capacity for humility. He was often brave, and then immediately afterward was a coward. This is why James 5:17 says, "Elijah was a human being, even as we are." Yet he is also considered one of the most amazing prophets in the Old Testament.

And then there's Rahab (her story starts in Joshua 2), another character from the Old Testament. She had been a prostitute—and she was a gentile. This was not a desired pedigree in her time and place, especially among the Israelites. And yet she and her family were the only survivors of Israel's conquest of Jericho. During the conflict, Rahab trusted God and protected Israelite spies in her home from the king of Jericho. After trusting God, saving their lives and risking her own, she cut a deal that protected her life and the lineage of her whole family. After the fall of Jericho, she was integrated into Israel and married Salmon. She became King David's great-great-grandmother, and part of Jesus's family tree. Yup, one of Jesus's grandmothers was a prostitute!

As these examples show, God is in the business of using people who are disqualified and transforming them with his love and grace.

I'm the father of five amazing kids, and I want them to be anchored to their role in the world as followers of Jesus. They are called to be people of influence—witnesses—and so are you. Acts 1:8 says, "But you will receive power when the Holy Spirit comes on you; and you will be my witnesses in Jerusalem, and in all Judea and Samaria, and to the ends of the earth." Witnesses testify to the truth of their experiences. They speak about what they see, hear, and do with the hope of influencing others to believe what they believe, or to have the same kinds of experiences they have had. As a Christian, Jesus gives you the power to be an influencer.

I will never forget the first time my son, Everett, came home from parkour lessons. He spent fifteen minutes explaining how he got to jump off a fourteen-foot wall. He told me all about trying to climb up the wall with limited grips, then jump off and land safely in a pile of foam blocks. His heart was pounding, his feet and hands were sweating, and he was nervous, scared, and elated all at the same time. When he finally jumped he felt like he was flying. After telling me all of this he said, "Dad, you should totally come with me and try it!" At six years old he was being a witness, testifying to his life-changing experience, in hopes that I would join him. He wasn't being coercive or manipulative; he wanted to share his joy with me.

As a young follower of Jesus, my hope is that you would find real joy in being a powerful influencer for him. That does not mean you will become an evangelist in the Billy Graham sense, but in your everyday words and actions you will be influencing the way people see Jesus. Everett had great joy in sharing his experience with me, but imagine if I had joined him the next week at parkour. The two of us together, fourteen feet in the air, ready to jump! He would be standing there, even more joyous than the first time, because someone he loved deeply was jumping with him. We would have forged a shared experience that drew us closer to each other.

You have been given unique talents, spiritual gifts, and a network of relationships that no one else possesses, all so that people might experience a part of Jesus through you, one that they would not be able to encounter anywhere else. As they experience Jesus the way you do, it will overwhelmingly increase your own joy in being a Jesus follower and draw you, and them, deeper into friendship with Jesus.

HOW TO READ THIS BOOK

The first section of this book will help you understand your identity. Finding identity is one of the biggest issues facing teenagers today. Often, the voices of the world tell you to simply adopt whatever behaviors, attitudes, and beliefs you like the best. But as a follower of Jesus, understanding your identity starts with thinking about "whose" you are. This section will invite you to look at your friendship with Jesus and how that friendship changes everything. You will discover the core elements of being a follower of Jesus, elements that you share in common with every believer, as well as the unique gifts he has given you.

The second section will focus on belonging. You will have the opportunity to think about how you belong, and how you have a mission set before you to help others belong in relationship with Jesus. One thing is true of all people: we desperately want to belong. We are creatures of community who fear nothing more than isolation and aloneness. Jesus talks directly about the unity of all believers, and the Bible is full of stories conveying the welcoming nature of Jesus toward all people—no matter who they are or what they have done. Everyone and anyone can be friends with Jesus, and his friends are all supposed to be friends with one another.

My son once said, "Dad, if we didn't love those we disagreed with, we wouldn't have any friends." He was right. Belonging is about more than liking people. It's about loving them beyond the differences.

Student leaders are given the opportunity to display the level of unity that Jesus prayed for in John 17. Hopefully, you'll finish this section knowing your gifts, understanding your role in the church, and relying on the Holy Spirit to use all of that to create communities of belonging where everyone can be friends with Jesus.

The third section focuses on creating. As a student leader you will be given the opportunity to lead something or someone. Leaders are creators by necessity. Leaders create systems, projects, plans, spaces, and opportunities. You will learn how you can help create the culture around you, one that leads to life transformation.

The only prerequisites to growing as a student leader are being willing to learn, keeping an open mind, and allowing Jesus to do something significant in your life and your community. As you learn and reflect, I think this book is best read alongside a few other people. Each chapter has reflection questions at the end added by my good friend Len Kageler. These questions are designed to help you process the information for personal application, but are best reflected on in an open, trusting conversation with your peers and pastor. If you can, I'd recommend going through them together in your student leadership meetings. Through others you will encounter different spiritual gifts, and therefore different aspects of Jesus himself. All of this will help you to solidify your identity, belong more fully to your community, and create opportunities for others to encounter Jesus meaningfully.

Dan Boal

Life's a Learning Curve

Student leaders are growing in knowing themselves and how God made them.

Have you ever found yourself asking these questions? *Who am I? Why do I exist? What is my purpose in life? Why do certain people like me when others do not? Does God love me? Does anyone love me? Why am I even asking these questions?* And the list goes on.

Your impulse to ask these questions is evidence of your desire to better understand your identity. As you learn more about your true self, it will provide you with purpose in your friendships, family, communities, and Jesus's greater plan for your life.

Let's think about identity in another context: your social media profile. Based on your viewing or clicking habits, social media sites make recommendations of videos for you to watch or product links for you to click on. They know how many cat videos you watch, and if you are more likely to watch those for fifteen minutes than a Twitch feed of epic fails, or vice versa. They want you to engage—to like, up-vote, share, comment, swipe, etc. Eventually, these sites know you well enough to recommend only the things that are likely to connect with you—and get you to spend more time on the site.

This type of profiling happens in real-world relationships and communities as well. Essentially, people create a profile on you in their minds based on your actions, statements, clothing, friendships, and factors such as race, gender, and where you live. These profiles can give you access, or restrict your access, to different groups. Often, your behaviors may shift, to greater or lesser degrees, from group to group as you go through your day. Let's say you love to sing. Your music class in public high school wouldn't expect you to stand up and sing worship songs on a Tuesday morning. On the other hand, your youth group might on Wednesday night. While singing is something you do in both groups, the person to whom the singing is directed is different. Your high school musical or choir concert is for an audience, and worship songs are for God. The question that's important to ask yourself is what things about you remain true in all settings and relationships? What is true of you in all contexts is your true identity. The true thing here is that you are a singer, and whether you're singing musicals or worship songs you view all acts of singing as part of your identity and worshipful to Jesus. After all, creating beautiful melodies and using this natural talent is a testimony to God's craftsmanship in your life.

I first began to struggle with my own identity in sixth grade. From kindergarten through fifth grade I attended a small private school in the suburbs of Philadelphia. I grew up with the same twenty-three kids in my class for my first six formative school years. I had three best friends and a certain sense of group belonging. When sixth grade came I had to make the transition to public middle school. All of the sudden I was thrust into an environment with 200 other sixth graders who were coming from multiple elementary schools. Each person was now charting a new identity course, trying to understand themselves in a new context among different people. In this maelstrom of transition, I lost a strong sense of who I was.

At the time there was a brand of clothing that was taking the middle school world by storm, FUBU. If you were a sixth grader and you could afford FUBU, you clearly had some social standing that others did not. FUBU stood for For Us, By Us, a brand of clothing popularized in urban black communities and idolized by my black friends. I remember going home and begging my parents to buy me a FUBU shirt, explaining to them how I wouldn't fit in without it. I was starting to make some friends who loved the brand, and I thought it would be a great "in." Thankfully my parents understood how I was feeling and took me out shopping that night. When I went to school the next day peacocking my new gear, I was astounded when one kid immediately made fun of me for wearing it. This guy wasn't part of the group I was trying to impress, he was one of the kids I used to be friends with the year before. He was making fun of me for wearing the clothes. On top of that, the group I was trying to impress didn't think it was anything special. I was discouraged, and later that day I went home reeling in despair. Why didn't I seem to fit in, despite my best efforts?

What I didn't understand at the time was that 200 other preteens were trying to find their place, just like I was. As I tried to find where I belonged, I was being pushed out of some circles and invited into others. Every other student was going through the same thing. We were all trying on new behaviors, attitudes, clothing, language, and friendships. I eventually did find a group that accepted me as part of their tribe. When I did it wasn't based on clothing, but on our ability to connect over shared values and experiences.

As a person you will always be in a state of emotional, cognitive, and spiritual formation. As a teenager, this state is heightened. There is greater change in a shorter period because you are part of so many friend groups, sports teams, workplaces, and other communities. Because of this, it's common to try on new behaviors until you find the ones that fit best.

Think about how many friends you have had in the past few years who seemed to change overnight into someone else, with new friends or attitudes or behaviors. Similar to going shopping and trying on clothes, we try on behaviors, practices, and belief systems for seasons of time, trying to understand who we really are. This is a very normal part of adolescence that each person experiences differently. It can be fun, exciting, possibly traumatizing, and can make you feel downright crazy, but if walked through wisely it is an important part of discovering a solid identity.

Throughout your life you will be discovering your true identity—the things that are true about you in all contexts and relationships. At the end of your life you will be as unique as a unicorn. There will be things that are true of you no matter what. The Latin word for that is *ipseity*, which means being the true you in all circumstances. The opposite of this is hypocrisy, which means being one thing in one context and something else in another. Part of becoming a spiritually mature follower of Jesus is living a life of *ipseity*.

Even unicorns have some universal truths they share in common with other unicorns. For starters, they all have a single corn. In the same way, there are some foundational parts of the identity of every follower of Jesus.

Know Who You Are and Whose You Are

YOU ARE FRIENDS WITH JESUS

In early elementary school it's common to find your first "best" friend. Usually around first or second grade you have that one close friend who would be heartbroken if you couldn't make it to her birthday party. Together you had your first overnight and stayed up as late as you could, sharing secrets you were sure—at seven years old—were incredibly deep and dark. You knew her favorite color and who her first big crush was, and you sat with each other as much as possible in school. At recess, you always played the same game and tried to be on the same team. Then one day, you got in a lot of trouble together. That is when you knew this was special. This person wasn't just any friend. This was your *best* friend.

This was your first experience of choosing to know someone and be known by them. Unlike a relationship with your parents, where you had no say in it, you chose this person and this person chose you back, out of all the kids in all the classes in all the schools.

Every day we are in process of making choices. Our most significant choices are the people we spend time with, and the types of relationships we have with them. The author of the book of Proverbs puts it this way: "The righteous choose their friends carefully..." (Proverbs 12:26). Choosing friends carefully is important, because our friends carry major influence in our lives. Have you ever known someone who changed because of who he chose to spend time with? Choosing to have someone in your life means choosing to give that person influence in shaping who you become.

These are powerful choices. There is vulnerability that comes with close friendship, and a deep bond of intimacy that grows over time as you share experiences and form a unique set of unspoken truths between you. Because of this, all of us place exceptionally high value on the relationships we choose. It's why we tend to get so defensive if our parents or others criticize our friends. It feels as if we are being criticized for the choices we've made.

With that in mind, let's think about the most meaningful relationship anyone can have: a relationship with Jesus. This relationship is based on choices too. After all, Jesus chose you. Just as Jesus chose to invite the disciples to come and follow him, Jesus chose to offer the same invitation to you, and at some point you chose him back. He wanted, and still wants, to be in a unified, intimate, close-knit relationship with you, and you decided that was worthwhile.

Jesus wants to be face-to-face friends with you. He desires for you to be with him here on earth, and with him eternally. He wants you to experience the fullness of his power, love, and awesomeness in your life. He prays that you would be so close to him you would experience his glory (John 17:24-26). He prays that you would be able to ask for anything you want in his name and have it (John 14:14).

As a student leader, everything starts with your relationship with Jesus. You are best friends. But like all relationships, it will take work. You may have chosen Jesus, but are you willing to be vulnerable with him? Are you willing to give Jesus full permission to influence who you will become?

YOU ARE SPIRITUALLY ALIVE

Becoming a follower of Jesus was the single most powerful experience of my life. I was seventeen years old and attending a Christian discipleship conference for teenagers. As a sermon waned to an end, I felt the distinct movement of the Holy Spirit pulling me toward the truth of my humanity: that in my sin I was separated from God the Father, but in his love he made a way for us to be reunited. This was the first time I really understood the gospel. This was the day when I chose to have faith that the atoning work of Jesus on the cross was sufficient to forgive me of my sin and reunite me with God. While once I was spiritually dead, on that day the grace of God allowed me to truly come to life.

Can you remember when you chose to become a follower of Jesus? Maybe you had a powerful encounter with the living God that brought about faith. Possibly your experience was gradual, and at some point along the way you realized you were convinced of the truth of the gospel. Or maybe you can't even remember when you chose to follow Jesus, you just always have. However you came to faith, before that time you were, as the apostle Paul so eloquently put it, "spiritually dead." I liken being spiritually dead to not being one hundred percent the person you were meant to be. Before you were a follower of Jesus, a key part of your identity was missing. As the apostle Paul shares with us in Ephesians 2:1-3,

> As for you, you were dead in your transgressions and sins, in which you used to live when you followed the ways of this world and of the ruler of the kingdom of the air, the spirit who is now at work in those who are disobedient. All of us also lived among them at one time, gratifying the cravings of our flesh and following its desires and thoughts. Like the rest, we were by nature deserving of wrath.

Simply put, before we followed Jesus, our brokenness was our primary identity. But the beautiful consequence of faith in Christ is that we are now spiritually alive. Jesus says it this way: "I have come that they may have life, and have it to the full" (John 10:10). This full life Jesus refers to is what really shows that we are now his followers. Instead of our identity being shaped by spiritual brokenness, it is now free to be shaped by the living Spirit of God.

When we read about Jesus having his last supper with the disciples we see a wonderfully intimate, yet painful, picture of what is essentially a living funeral. If you have attended a funeral or wake, you can probably recall the emotions present. They range from oppressive feelings of loss to even great relief and joy. Often, before someone passes away that person will write a last will and testament. This legal document describes a person's final wishes: what he would like to have happen to his possessions, and desires for his celebration of life or funeral. All of this is often meant to bring some consolation to the living.

At the last supper, Jesus gives a verbal last will and testament describing the inheritance that will come to anyone who chooses to be his disciple: the Holy Spirit.

> "But the Advocate, the Holy Spirit, whom the Father will send in my name, will teach you all things and will remind you of everything I have said to you. Peace I leave with you; my peace I give you." (John 14:26-27)

When we are spiritually dead, we are guided by our spiritually broken, untrue selves. In this state, our actions can steal joy, kill relationships, and do all sorts of damage. But Jesus gives us the Holy Spirit, which brings us the actual peace of God. Remember, Jesus declares, "Peace I leave with you; my peace I give you." As a spiritually alive follower of Jesus, you are able to follow the Holy Spirit, and the Spirit will transform your heart and your motives, helping you make decisions that bring about the peace of Jesus. This is life and life to the full, the ability to follow a living God, find freedom from sin, and do what is right.

YOU ARE A CHILD OF GOD

A few years ago I was visiting the southern region of Burkina Faso, Africa. We traveled through the bush for six painstaking hours to visit the village with the highest infant mortality rate. At the time, our student ministry was engaged in a humanitarian project to bring clean water wells to villages like this one so that physical needs could be addressed, and spiritual doors opened. In Burkina Faso seventy-two out of every one thousand births ended with the child dying in infancy[1], and according to our hosts only four out of ten children made it past age ten. The lack of access to medical care, the poor nutrition, and the scarcity of food, coupled with dark brown drinking water filled with parasites and polution, are the primary factors in the death rate.

Our leaders, from a mission agency named Envision, had not been to this village in several years. We were going with the hope of negotiating a land contract on which we could drill a well for them. Our intention was to meet with the village chief. Instead we were met by hundreds of families bringing us their children. The translator informed us that these parents were offering their children to us. At first, I thought this was because they wanted better lives for their children, but I was told it was because the families were actually better off without them. One less child meant one less mouth to feed, and these parents knew these children were likely to die anyway.

I looked at the mass of people and was overwhelmed with compassion. I wanted to take every child home, but the need was too great. It took everything I had to inform these desperate people that I had no way to care for their children. Every time I looked into their eyes and said, "I can't take your child" or "I'm not allowed to take your child," I knew I was essentially issuing that child an early death sentence.

In this moment I was hit with a stark spiritual reality. The world we live in is filled with people who have a spiritual death sentence. They lack access to the truth of the gospel. They are drinking from the polluted waters of the world, looking for life and finding only sickness. This is the world Jesus entered.

Throughout the New Testament account of Jesus's ministry you will see some version of this phrase: "…and Jesus looked at the crowd and was filled with compassion." His compassion comes from a love that leads to action, and was born out of God's own compassion for all lost people. It was compassion that led Jesus to create a way for us to become God's spiritual sons and daughters.

Jesus is the only one capable of adopting the whole world, and the only one who can give us spiritual life. Jesus came into the world and chose us as his children. As Paul says, "God decided in advance to adopt us into his own family by bringing us to himself through Jesus Christ. This is what he wanted to do, and it gave him great pleasure" (Ephesians 1:5, NLT). It broke my heart to say no to those children in Burkina Faso, but it gives God great pleasure to never have to say no to anyone who asks to become his child. He decided that he was going to make everyone his spiritual son and daughter—including you.

John says, "But to all who believed him and accepted him, he gave the right to become children of God" (John 1:12, NLT). When you are adopted you inherit the full privileges of any blood-born son or daughter. We often are confronted by our own brokenness, which can lead to guilt and the feeling that we don't deserve the love of God, but nothing is further from the truth. Like Jesus, we too are children of God. He cares for us, loves us, and provides us with everything we need to have rich spiritual lives.

Jesus calls us to himself, saying, "Let the children come to me. Don't stop them! For the Kingdom of Heaven belongs to those who are like these children" (Matthew 19:14, NLT). As a child of God, the kingdom of God is yours. You are an adopted son or daughter. This is the core of your new identity.

Too often we find our identity in temporary or situational things. If we like music, we might find our identity in a type of music or band. If we are into technology, we may find our identity with a group of people or a certain technological science that piques our interest. Is it wrong to find affinity with these groups? Absolutely not. But if our interests are the primary factors determining who we believe ourselves to be, then we are placing ourselves on uncertain ground. The core of our identity must be found in things that are unchangeable.

Jesus wants you to look to him for help in understanding who God made you to be. Jesus chose you to be his friend. Through this friendship you have become spiritually alive. You are a child of God, with the same privileges as any child. Regardless of what you have done or will do, you are deeply known and deeply loved.

YOU ARE A DISCIPLE OF JESUS

Close friends start to share a lot in common. A few years ago, I found myself part of a running joke with my closest ministry friend, Clayton. Weekly we would come into the office wearing very similar, if not identical, outfits. At first it was funny, symbolic of our close friendship and shared taste in somewhat fashionable Target apparel. But as time went on, the occurrences became more regular than I care to admit. One of us would usually end up changing our shirt during our lunch break.

When we are close friends with someone, we begin to share similar attributes. We start to like the same things, like clothes and music. We often take on similar behaviors and phrases of speech. Think of your closest friend. Chances are you can identify ways in which you mimic one another. Sometimes it's cute and fun. Other times, you can see the negative impact of that relationship.

If you are close friends with Jesus, sooner or later you will begin to mimic Jesus. You will think like he did, do what he did, and spend time with God the Father the way he did. There is a phrase I once heard that I have adopted as my own: "If it was normal for Jesus, then it should be normal for you." So, what was normal for Jesus? When I ask this question the first response I get is usually a list of all the miraculous things Jesus did. This is an easy place to start. However, there were many behaviors of Jesus that should be normal for our everyday lives.

To understand what Jesus did, we must go back to the first century in the ancient Near East. This is the culture in which Jesus grew up and lived. Specifically, he lived in first century Jewish ancient Near East culture, and was from the town of Galilee, which had its own unique expressions of the Jewish faith. All of this being the case, Jesus had unique life experiences.

Given the time in history in which he lived and the city he was from, Jesus most likely went to a school at the local synagogue. At age five, Jesus would have begun memorizing the Torah, the first five books of the Bible. Through age ten, like the other boys and girls, he would have memorized, line for line and word for word, Genesis through Deuteronomy. This is why Jesus was later able to teach from memory. He had studied these words every day. At this time books were rare and expensive. They were technically scrolls, and the process of making scroll paper was so time-consuming and costly that books were luxuries most people couldn't afford. They were stored at the synagogue, and a daily journey there to study and memorize the Word of God was common practice.

At age ten, Jesus would have undergone a test by a rabbi—a Jewish scholar or teacher of the laws and interpretations of the Torah. After passing the test, he would have entered the second phase of school, known as "oral Torah." There, young boys would work on interpreting the Old Testament and how to use it to follow God. According to custom, female students would not have been permitted to advance further in their education of the Torah. They would have been asked to learn the trades of their mothers, and would commonly have become clothiers, weavers, or homemakers.

From around age twelve through about age twenty or thirty, Jesus would have continued his education in oral Torah, and would also have begun to pursue the trade of his father. Jesus's trade was carpentry.

At thirty years old, if one was considered an excellent teacher, that person could begin a teaching ministry in his community. This explains why Jesus began his ministry at thirty years old. At this point he was seen as someone who could teach with authority. Jesus was now a rabbi.

At this time, there were two types of rabbis. First, the rabbi of the Torah. This person could teach current interpretations of the Law. Just like your high school teacher, who can only teach approved and proven concepts, so the rabbi of the Torah could only teach what had been approved by institutions above him. The second class of rabbi was the rabbi of the *semikhah*. This rabbi could teach new interpretations of the law, finding meaning no one else had found in the text before. Jesus was a rabbi of the second type.

Jesus's words often signal that he is teaching a new interpretation of Scripture. "You have heard it said…" he says when introducing an idea, continuing, "…but I say…" In other words, *I give you a new interpretation*. Let's look at a few examples.

"You have heard that it was said, *'You shall not commit adultery.'* **But I tell you** *that anyone who looks at a woman lustfully has already committed adultery with her in his heart"* (Matthew 5:27-28, emphasis added).

"**It has been said,** *'Anyone who divorces his wife must give her a certificate of divorce.* **But I tell you** *that anyone who divorces his wife, except for sexual immorality, makes her the victim of adultery, and anyone who marries a divorced woman commits adultery"* (Matthew 5:31-32, emphasis added).

"You have heard that it was said, *'Eye for eye, and tooth for tooth.'* **But I tell you,** *do not resist an evil person. If anyone slaps you on the right cheek, turn to them the other cheek also"* (Matthew 5:38-39, emphasis added).

These are the words of a rabbi who taught with authority, stating what was commonly accepted and then interpreting a deeper understanding.

When this type of rabbi started a teaching ministry, he would invite young men to come and learn under him. The rabbi would say, "*Lech Acharai*," which means "Come follow me." A young man in this place and time who heard these words from a rabbi would drop everything to go and learn under this person.

This explains why the twelve disciples left their current occupations as fishermen, tax collectors, etc., to follow this rabbi, Jesus. In that time and place, being invited to follow a rabbi was the equivalent of being given a full-ride scholarship to an Ivy League school.

Those who followed would leave behind all that they knew and had been doing before, but they were promised an amazing future as respected religious leaders and teachers, the most desired role in their community. Those who followed a rabbi were called disciples, and they would literally follow the rabbi wherever he went, living according to his interpretations of the Torah and trying to imitate him in all of his actions. Everything in a disciple's life came second to learning from the rabbi, and living like the rabbi lived.

This is why Peter, upon seeing Jesus walk on water, says, "Lord, if it's you…tell me to come to you on the water." Jesus says to come, and Peter gets out of the boat and walks on the water toward Jesus (Matthew 14:27-29). The reason Peter knew he could walk on water was that his rabbi was walking on water. It was the commonsense thing for him to do, even if to us it seems pretty astounding. (Can you imagine being one of the other disciples on the boat? For the first thirty seconds you would have watched Jesus and Peter, kicking your sandals off getting ready to jump overboard. As soon as you saw Peter sink—because he does start to doubt, and to sink—you would have strapped them back on.)

As we become friends with Jesus, do we assume, like the twelve disciples, that we can do the things he did? Are we asking ourselves what those things are? Do we have the faith to follow him, even when it doesn't seem to make sense?

Jesus was a rabbi and the disciples were his students. Yet, the relationship Jesus established with his disciples was more than that. It was one of deep friendship. We see that in the words Jesus says in John 15:15: "I no longer call you servants, because a servant does not know his master's business. Instead, I have called you friends, for everything that I learned from my Father I have made known to you."

Even after Jesus's death and resurrection, the Bible is full of stories of the disciples continuing on in the ministry of Jesus. Jesus gave the disciples, his students and friends, the authority to do what he did. He does the same for us today.

Discipleship is at the heart of friendship with Jesus. If we are friends with Jesus, then we can and should do the same things Jesus did. Why? Because we accepted the call to follow him. Just like the disciples in the New Testament, we too are being asked to leave our old lives behind and mimic the life of Jesus. So if it was normal for Jesus, it should be normal for you.

YOU HAVE A LIFESTYLE TO EMBRACE
The Practices of Jesus, and Behaviors of a Disciple
If we want to be like Jesus, we have to do the things Jesus did. If we are going to allow him to have life-shaping influence in our lives, then we must create spaces for ourselves to become face-to-face friends with Jesus. Let's look at some ways to do that.

Jesus Prayed in Private
Prayer is often a misunderstood concept, but at its heart, prayer is simply talking to God. We can pray publicly, or with a small group of others at church or at home, or on our own in a private, one-on-one conversation with God.

Many teenagers (and even many adults) are hesitant to spend extended time in private prayer. Many of us learned to pray through the example of others. We saw and experienced structured times of prayer in church, at youth group, or at home. Public prayer is valuable, but it is different from private prayer. Structured, public prayer is less intimate. Think about the most private conversations you have had with your friends. Would you have ever had those conversations in public? No. They were meant to remain private. Sharing intimate conversations with trusted friends increases your sense of closeness and loyalty.

We can't expect to have a deep, close, and trusting relationship with God unless we take time to talk with him in private. Jesus modeled this for all believers, both by his example and through his words. This, for instance, is how he instructs the disciples to pray:

"And when you pray, do not be like the hypocrites, for they love to pray standing in the synagogues and on the street corners to be seen by others. Truly I tell you, they have received their reward in full. But when you pray, go into your room, close the door and pray to your Father, who is unseen. Then your Father, who sees what is done in secret, will reward you." (Matthew 6:5-6)

Jesus was often found alone in prayer with God; the Bible is full of examples. To list just a few, he prayed at his baptism (Luke 3:21), during times of retreat from his public teaching ministry (Luke 5:16), before walking on water (Matthew 14:22-23, Mark 6:46, John 6:15), before choosing the twelve disciples (Luke 6:12), and before teaching his disciples the Lord's Prayer (Luke 11:1). Jesus's private prayer life is always followed by incredible public ministry.

In his book *How to Pray*[2], R. A. Torrey notes that Jesus prayed early in the morning as well as all night, that he prayed both before and after the great events of his life, and that he prayed "when life was unusually busy."

If Jesus spent this much time in one-on-one conversation with God, we should do the same. Private prayer gives us spaces where we can not only talk to God, but where we can also listen to the direction he might have for our lives.

Jesus Fasted

What is fasting? There are many kinds of fasts. People fast from social media, certain foods, and really snarky people may fast from fasting. While all types of fasting can have value, fasting from food is the model we are given in the Bible, and a model we should embrace. Fasting, in the Biblical sense, is the purposeful choice not to eat for a specific amount of time so that you are able to hear God more clearly. Every time you get a hunger pang, it reminds you that the thing you need most in life is not food but the presence of God.

Jesus puts it this way: "It is written: 'Man shall not live on bread alone, but on every word that comes from the mouth of God'" (Matthew 4:4). When you fast, you are emotionally, physically, and cognitively recognizing that more than you need a meal right now, you need God to feed your soul, maybe with answers to prayer, wisdom for your life, or the presence of his Spirit.

In Matthew 4, before he embarks on a mission to literally change the world, Jesus spends forty days in the desert fasting. If Jesus, who was God but also fully man, found fasting helpful, we would also be wise to fast.

Fasting done well is not a weight loss plan or a fast track for getting closer to Jesus. It is supposed to be one of our spiritual disciplines. Jesus teaches on fasting in Matthew 6:5-13 and instructs that those who fast should do so as an act of private worship between you and God.

A few years ago I fasted for three days. I was seeking a specific answer to prayer. I began the fast not knowing how long it would last. On the third day I felt Jesus release me from fasting when a friend asked me to lunch. I didn't get the answer I wanted before I ended my fast, but I was pleased to have spent those days letting my hunger pangs draw me closer to Jesus. Jesus's presence gave me peace even though I didn't get an answer.

Jesus will never take you into unhealthy extremes when fasting. Fasting is an act of worship, something that draws us toward Jesus. Are you willing to spend time without eating, just like Jesus did, in order to be close with God? If you want to learn more about fasting, talk with a trusted adult.

Jesus Knew the Bible and Had It Memorized

Spending time in the Bible can be a difficult task. If you grew up in the church, then you have heard numerous stories from the Bible throughout your life. When you go to read the Bible, it can feel old and monotonous. It's like watching a rerun for the thirtieth time.

There is also a language barrier. Most of us are not fluent in Greek, Hebrew, or Aramaic, the three languages in which the original manuscripts of the Bible were written. Also, there are many translations of the Bible in English that use vocabulary that can be difficult to understand. While the King James version is the original English translation, the way it's written makes it complicated for readers in the twenty-first century to understand. (Although it does use the word *unicorn* nine times to describe spiritual creatures. How cool is that?)

Others avoid reading the Bible because they are too busy and haven't created space in their lives for reading. And some people just don't understand what they are reading, because they feel 2,000 or more years removed from the events the Bible depicts.

And yet, we know Jesus spent time with the Bible. If we want to be like him, we should too. Jesus regularly refers to Scripture. Throughout his ministry Jesus quotes Genesis, Exodus, Leviticus, Deuteronomy, Isaiah, Hosea, Micah, Malachi, Jeremiah, Zechariah, the Psalms, and Daniel. (Right now, you may be wondering why he only quoted the Old Testament. I'm going to give you a minute to figure that out.) Jesus paraphrases Bible passages, and he also quotes them word for word.

Sometimes, I play a game with student leaders, asking them to name as many brand slogans as they can. Within sixty seconds they'll come up with dozens. (My personal favorite is for KitKat, which ends with "Break me off a piece of that KitKat bar!" This jingle is simple and repetitive, easy to remember. Whoever wrote it clearly had a stroke of jingle genius.)

After they've named dozens of jingles, I ask student leaders to quote the Bible as many times as they can in one minute. Usually, they come up with half as many Bible quotes as jingles, or even less. This simple exercise indicates the biblical illiteracy of the crowd. I don't do this to shame them, just to emphasize that we remember more about the things with which we spend more time.

Jesus spent a lot of time in God's Word. How much time do you spend in the Word of God?

Jesus modeled for us that prayer, fasting, and time spent reading and memorizing the Word of God are foundational practices of a disciple. These spiritual practices create space for us to encounter the living Jesus and spend real time with him, giving him influence in our lives. They help us to hear Jesus affirming our identity. We are his friends. We have been forgiven and are now spiritually alive, adopted sons and daughters of God. We are people who hear the words of the Father and know his heart.

Reflection Questions: Know Who You Are and Whose You Are

1. We all lean on certain things to provide our identity. Other than your Christian faith, what are two or three things that have helped create your identity (for example, good grades, basketball, high school band, etc.)?

2. When and how did you come to a personal relationship/ friendship with Jesus?

3. If a camera crew followed you around for a typical day, from the moment you woke up until the time you went to bed, and that sixteen-hour movie was shown to a group of strangers (happily eating free popcorn or chicken wings), what evidence would they see that you are a disciple of Jesus?

4. Who, outside of your youth group, has been or is a good model for you of what it means to be a disciple of Jesus?

Know the Power of Your Identity

VICTORY IS YOURS

Have you ever met someone who likes to lose? Of course not. It is in our nature to want to win.

Watching my kids go through the toddler years has allowed me to see the fundamental human desire to be winners. Currently, my kids play a game they call "goo-goo." I can't actually figure out the rules to this game, but it's obvious that being the "goo-goo" is not good. My son, who is the oldest, complains incessantly when he has to be the "goo-goo" and always tries to manipulate the game to avoid it.

Have you ever wondered why we so desperately want to be winners? I think it is because on some level we know that we, via our ancestors, lost the most precious thing we ever had: eternal life with face-to-face communion with God in the garden of Eden. Ever since that moment, humans have been searching for ways to be winners again.

Every day, athletes, politicians, movie stars, and even pastors try desperately to make a lasting impact on the world, an impact that will outlive them. On some level we all know that death is coming, and as a result we work tirelessly (often subconsciously) to create for ourselves reputations as winners that will last even after we are gone.

The Bible is filled with stories of victory. Victory in battles, victory over sickness, victory over political enemies, victories of oppressed people, and most importantly, victory over sin and death. The unique thing about the victories in the Bible is that they are never achieved by human effort. Try as they might, the people of Scripture only attain victory when the Lord gives it to them. The same is true of us. In our own strength, we will never achieve victory over temptation, sin, or death.

This is important to remember when you serve as a student leader. People often get stuck in repeat patterns of sin, but Jesus wants more for us. As he says in John 10:10, "The thief comes only to steal and kill and destroy; I have come that they may have life, and have it to the full."

When we are stuck in sin, shame, guilt, loneliness, isolation, depression, anxiety, or anything else that is the result of sin and brokenness, we are not living life to the full. As Jesus said in John 16:33, "I have overcome the world." The original manuscript of this verse was written in Greek, and the Greek word *nikao* is the word we translate into *overcome*. *Nikao* literally means "victor" or "victory." (*Nikao* is the same word that Nike originates from.) Jesus is saying he is the victory, the conqueror of all things. It is only by his power that we can have the kind of victory that can bring "life to the full" on this earth.

Because we are imperfect, there will always be opportunities for Jesus to help you achieve victory. As a friend of Jesus, your job is to constantly ask and desire Jesus to reveal to you the areas in your life where you are experiencing spiritual, emotional, and physical loss. Then, ask Jesus to conquer these issues so that you may see him as the victor in your life. Now is the time to claim victory, in Jesus's name, over anything that is keeping you from life and life to the full.

GOD IS MAKING YOU SPECIAL
Have you ever heard of the seven wonders of the world? These are

ancient creations, like the pyramids in Giza, Egypt, that were made by humans and which were truly marvelous in their day. Given the technology and the rudimentary sciences and mathematic principals available at the time they were built, they're especially impressive. And yet there is nothing quite as marvelous as the capstone of God's creative work: human beings.

We could spend a long time marveling about the complexities of the human body—the design is amazing—but to me the even greater miracle is the one of individuality. Not only did God create billions of human beings who all look different, but each of us is also unique in heart, mind, and personality. There has never been, nor will there ever be, anyone like you.

Life experiences have a huge impact on the people we become. Some of them are good or great or even amazing, and some of them are absolutely miserable. And yet even the miserable experiences are key to God's plan to develop our individuality.

As a teenager growing up in Pennsylvania, every summer I had to spend two to three days spreading mulch around our property. It always seemed like my mom would wait until the hottest days of July and then order an actual dump truck of mulch to be dropped off at the house. Mulch is this combination of shredded wood, soil, and manure. It is very dense, heavy, dirty, and itchy. When you spread it over a flower bed it looks sharp and clean, but it is awful to work with. Every summer I hated seeing that dump truck arrive, knowing it meant several days of my life would be stolen for manual labor.

Then, one summer I had an opportunity to go on an eight-week mission trip to the beautiful state of Ohio. I was going to get out of having to mulch our property. Sure, I would be doing other work, but I wouldn't be doing *that* work. The purpose of this trip was to encourage local churches in rural communities by doing service projects and hosting outreach events. It was going to be a great trip— or so I thought.

I learned a valuable lesson about one week into the trip. If a big blue bus of thirty high schoolers rolls up to your church and you need to give them a service project to do, you might decide to have them spread mulch around your property. At church after church, for eight long weeks, I spread mulch, the very thing I'd been excited to escape. However, because I was the only person on my team who had experience mulching, I was able to use what I knew to make the work quite a bit easier and more efficient, and help the team work smarter, not harder. By the end of the summer I was managing most of our outdoor and landscaping projects. Before this trip, I didn't realize God had used my previous time spreading mulch to develop skills I could later use to teach others. I wouldn't have been able lead and teach those skills had I not first put in the hard work myself.

Sometimes God allows you to have experiences that are miserable in the moment, but are critical to shaping your skills and talents for his glory. Romans 8:28 says, "And we know that in all things God works for the good of those who love him, who have been called according to his purpose." You have been called for a special purpose, and because he loves you, God will work in your life and make meaning from your life experiences.

YOU ARE BECOMING A PERSON OF COMPASSION

In our desire to be winners, we set for ourselves high and sometimes lofty ambitions. These ambitions are often described in softer terms, like dreams, desires, or goals. Whatever you call it, every person has ambition. It is part of our human nature to see a mountain and want to climb it.

Speaking to a crowd in Houston, Texas, in 1962, President John F. Kennedy gave what has become a famous speech with the tagline "We choose to go to the moon," in which he declares that the United States will put the first man on the moon by the end of the decade. If you watch a YouTube video of this speech, people begin to scream and cheer. Why? Because people like to accomplish big things.

Ambition exists within the church as much as anywhere else. We have ambitions to be elders, teachers, or worship leaders, to attend an event, go on a mission trip, or take part in a camp weekend. Without ambition or drive, we wouldn't reach out and try to get what we want. When our ambitions work for our good and the good of others, they are beneficial and they move us forward. When left unchecked, our ambitions can become selfish and even harmful.

If we take the time to thoughtfully reflect, we may find that at times our ambitions are not pure, clean, or even honoring to God or other people. Jeremiah 17:9 addresses our human nature, saying, "The heart is deceitful above all things and beyond cure. Who can understand it?" This passage serves as a warning about our ambition. Do we really understand the motives behind what we want or why we are doing what we are doing?

We can tell that our ambitions have gone off track when we start to feel entitled to our goals or wants. If you find yourself saying about something, "I deserve it," that sentiment reflects a sense of entitlement. Entitlement is spoiled ambition.

I once heard someone say, "being selfless is actually an act of selfishness." This person explained the statement with a question: if you have a desire to serve others, are you doing it for their good, or are you *actually* motivated by the way you'll feel after being helpful? This person argued that the real reason we help others is not because they need help, but because it makes us feel good and fulfilled when we do. At first, I thought this person wasn't making any sense. Yet, the more I examined this statement and reflected on my own life, the more I realized it carried quite a bit of truth.

As a student leader it is easy to jump into all kinds of service opportunities with the church. We can agree to come early, stay late, serve at every function, and generally become "the rock star" leader in the student ministry. There is nothing wrong with wanting to be highly involved. But understanding our motivation is important. When we commit to everything because our ambition is to be noticed, appreciated, or in charge, we have ceased to serve the people and have started serving ourselves.

Jesus was well aware of the temptation of selfish ambition. It's why he declares boldly in Matthew 20:26-28,

> "whoever wants to become great among you must be your servant, and whoever wants to be first must be your slave—just as the Son of Man did not come to be served, but to serve, and to give his life as a ransom for many."

I love how Jesus calls it like it is. His own disciples fought and bickered over what they thought were leadership positions within the budding movement of Christ followers. Jesus recognizes this tendency in us, and Jesus tells us that we must seek not our own benefit but, always, the benefit of others. This is the complete opposite of what our human nature pushes us to do.

Throughout the New Testament, we see numerous times when Jesus is described as acting out of compassion. Compassion is love that motivates to action—specifically action that benefits others with no gain for ourselves. This always benefits God's kingdom, because compassionate actions bring about a reshaping of someone's life in a way that brings glory to God.

Jesus acted in compassion when he performed miracles and when he fed the 5,000 (Matthew 9:36). Jesus acted with compassion when he cast out demons and healed the sick (Mark 1:41; Luke 7:11-13). And Jesus expected his people to live in such a way that they also would be known for their compassion toward one another (John 13:35). Compassion is the defining characteristic of a Christian leader. Compassion marks us as people who serve those around us with genuine love. When we find ourselves seeking our own interests or focusing on what we "deserve," we have forgotten the very nature of Jesus, which is to have a heart that seeks first and foremost the benefit of others.

YOU WILL HAVE IDEAS FOR THE KINGDOM

If we are going to do what Jesus did, then we have to see people the way Jesus sees them. Every person, regardless of status, gifting, and talents, matters to God, and he wants us all to participate in his mission to redeem the world.

When you serve as a leader, you are going to have ideas that can advance the kingdom. They are birthed out of your uniqueness, gifts, experiences, natural talents, and passions. Unfortunately, not everyone is going to agree with your ideas. When there are disagreements, it's possible to begin seeing people as problems to be solved rather than partners in the kingdom. As a leader it is your responsibility and calling to launch all the people you lead into the mission of Jesus, regardless of their personality type, skillset, or how you think they fit with your vision of your church or ministry.

A few years ago I was redeveloping the ministry at my church. I had spent two years building a very specific programmatic structure, recruiting the right leaders and empowering gifted youth. I had a list of action steps I thought would help people encounter Jesus and experience life change. The plan seemed to be working in one sense, because increasing numbers of people were becoming part of our ministry. The problem was that the rigid structure I'd created didn't leave room for people to serve unless they met the very specific criteria for leadership I'd defined.

I had one leader—let's call him Pete—who was constantly breaking the structure of the ministry in order to disciple teenagers "his way." Frustrated, I called him in for a meeting. I felt I had to make a clear ultimatum: if Pete didn't change his course of action he would be dismissed from serving in the student ministry. Pete had become a problem to be solved.

Pete was not happy. He didn't understand why I would be upset that his small group of peers was engaging deeply with the Word of God, praying weekly for their friends, and actively engaged in their pursuit of being like Jesus. I tried explaining the reasons for the structure I had built. I failed to grasp that ultimately we both wanted the same thing, but we differed in how to get there.

He argued that my structure didn't work for the teenagers in his group, who were thriving within his structure. We went back and forth for about thirty minutes. In the end, I drew a hard line and Pete refused to cross it, saying he would stop serving in the ministry.

I wasn't sure how we got to that point, but I know I drove us there. I was convinced that my model and vision were right, and that if I could solve the problem of Pete the ministry would be better. I was upset that Pete didn't see the value of what I had built. I thought Pete was messing this whole thing up.

In reality, Pete was right on point. His ministry structure was better for his group. Within three weeks of ministry with my structure instead of Pete's, the youth from his group stopped coming all together. I quickly realized that my ambitions for the ministry were way more about me than about helping people actually be more like Jesus. When we are very passionate about our ideas, the danger is that we can lose sight of other people's gifts, callings, and talents. The apostle Paul says, "Now you are the body of Christ, and each one of you is a part of it" (1 Corinthians 12:27). If I was truly seeing Pete the way Jesus did I would have realized sooner that I would serve him and those youth best by finding a way for them to participate in the mission of Jesus, even if it wasn't exactly following the plan I'd created.

Thankfully, Pete and I had a chance to reconcile a few weeks later. We mutually apologized to one another over coffee. Me for my arrogance, and him for his stubbornness. Together we prayed that God would keep doing his beautiful work of transformation in the lives of the youth we both cared about and in our own lives.

Launching people into the mission of Jesus is messy. It won't always look the way we expect. Now as I work with people I try to embrace all of the ideas they suggest. They won't all fit into the structures I have built, but they all fit in the kingdom, which is infinitely bigger than me. I have learned that my role is to help leaders live out the dreams God has placed on their hearts, whether this means assisting them to do that within my structure or helping them create their own.

As a student leader, you have your own passions and gifts, and you will often have ideas that you'll want to run by your youth leader. This is a very good thing. Sometimes your youth leader will say yes, but she might also tell you no. She isn't saying no because she doesn't believe in your idea, but because it may not fit the structure of the existing ministry or one hundred percent align with the mission of your local church. The mature response is to try and understand from your leader's perspective the long-term impact of your idea. Is your idea potentially divisive? What are some relational potholes you'll need to navigate if you want this idea to work? Does your idea exclude some people? What kind of personnel and financial resources will it require? Could there be a different way to follow through on your idea without disrupting the current structure? A good approach is to start the conversation with, "I have this idea, and with your permission I would like to take full ownership of developing it within our youth group, and I'd love for you to help me think about ways we can make it work."

With an open mind, our God-given talents and passions can work together for more kingdom wins. God is asking you to create and go forth to participate in the mission of Jesus as you are gifted and called. This can happen when people are no longer problems to be solved, but friends we can partner with.

YOU ARE GIFTED
The Difference Between God-Given Talents and Spiritual Gifts

Have you ever played the game Hidden Talents? You go around the circle and share a unique talent you possess, and learn some strange and interesting things about the people in the group. I had a person who could squirt fluid from the tear duct near his left eyeball like a squirt gun, and another who could swallow anything and instantly, without vomiting, regurgitate it. Other youth have been phenomenal Manga comic artists and poets. You will quickly learn that everyone has some sort of innate talent.

God gave you natural talents as well as spiritual gifts. In your role as a student leader it's important to understand which are which. Natural talents are talents you were born with or acquired over the years— things like having an easy ability to understand music and play an instrument. Spiritual gifts, on the other hand, are supernatural. These are gifts that were given to you by the Holy Spirit when you became a follower of Jesus. The apostle Paul says,

> A spiritual gift is given to each of us so we can help each other. To one person the Spirit gives the ability to give wise advice; to another the same Spirit gives a message of special knowledge. The same Spirit gives great faith to another, and to someone else the one Spirit gives the gift of healing. He gives one person the power to perform miracles, and another the ability to prophesy. He gives someone else the ability to discern whether a message is from the Spirit of God or from another spirit. Still another person is given the ability to speak in unknown languages, while another is given the ability to interpret what is being said. It is the one and only Spirit who distributes all these gifts. He alone decides which gift each person should have. (1 Corinthians 12:7-11, NLT)

Let's examine some key aspects of natural talents and spiritual gifts.

Talents Are Inherited or Learned, but Gifts Are Received

This may be the most important difference. Natural talents are those abilities inherited from one's parents and nurtured in the context of one's family, or talents acquired by hard work, trial and error. Certain lines of talent, like athleticism or skill as a writer, can be passed down from one generation to the next.

This passing on and nurturing of talents has been common practice since the beginning of time. Today, many people of European descent have last names that reflect the natural talents of their lineage: Farmer, Archer, Potter, Baker, Hunter, and the list could go on.

Everyone Has Talents, but Only Christians Have Spiritual Gifts

The Holy Spirit of God resides in each and every follower of Jesus, and this Spirit is the source of spiritual gifts that dwell in us. Followers of Jesus have more than natural talents—we have supernatural gifts that allow us to participate in the spiritual world. The gifts of the Spirit can be used when you want to make a change in the spiritual world around you. Some of gifts that are common for followers of Jesus are wisdom, knowledge, faith (extraordinary trust and surrender), healing, the effecting of miracles, prophecy, the distinguishing of spirits (knowing if someone is preaching the truth according to the Spirit of God and the Bible), tongues (speaking in other languages without having studied them), the ability to interpret tongues (understanding a language you have never studied), service, teaching, exhortation (motivating someone to do something for Jesus), giving, leadership, mercy, apostleship, evangelism, and pastoral care (the desire to guide and nurture people in their spiritual development). Scripture mentions all of these by name, but that doesn't mean these are the only spiritual gifts.

You may be wondering why so many of these gifts sound like natural talents. After all, people who don't follow Jesus can also be merciful, serve, and be great leaders. How can you tell if something is a spiritual gift? First, a spiritual gift is something you didn't come by naturally, but have gained since becoming a follower of Jesus. Second, using a spiritual gift makes a spiritual difference in a spiritual world. The apostle Paul says in Ephesians 6:12, "For our struggle is not against flesh and blood, but against the rulers, against the authorities, against the powers of this dark world and against the spiritual forces of evil in the heavenly realms." If this is the case, then we would need spiritual weapons. These gifts are the tools needed to participate in the mission of Jesus, and they are powerful enough to overcome evil.

Natural Talents Can Serve the Self, but Spiritual Gifts Only Serve God's Purposes

When you become self-focused or overly ambitious, your natural talents become the foundations on which you build your life. You can exercise natural talents in ways that lead to your personal gain, even at the expense of others. On the other hand, when you embrace your calling to be a person of compassion, you may use some of your natural talents, but you will *always* use your spiritual gifts. When you use your spiritual gifts "for the common good" and to the glory of God, you make a difference in the spiritual world around you. Where there is darkness you bring light. Where there are lies you bring truth.

Where there is confusion you bring clarity. Where there is a need you fill it. When someone needs to hear the gospel you share it with him or her. As you act out of compassion using your spiritual gifts, you will see hearts and minds change. People who were once lost will become found.

Just like your natural talents, spiritual gifts can grow and mature. The more you put your spiritual gifts into practice, the more God will use them.

Reflection Questions: Know the Power of Your Identity

1. This chapter mentioned several positive things that we are becoming as followers of Jesus. Which do you relate to, and why?
    - Victory is yours
    - God is making you special
    - You are becoming a person of compassion
    - You can see people like Jesus sees them
    - You are gifted

2. Which of the above is most difficult for you, and why might that be?

3. If you are discussing this chapter with a group, take a moment to consider the person sitting on your right. Tell the rest of the group what you think this person is best at from the five things mentioned in the chapter. After all have shared around the circle, you could offer prayers of thanks to God for the good you see in each other. Put everyone's name in a hat, everyone draws one name, and that is the person you thank God for now in prayer. All pray one at a time around the circle.

3 Know Your Humanity

WE ALL HAVE SPIRITUALLY DEFECTIVE DNA

The phrase "spiritually defective DNA"[3] is not meant to be the kind of term you'd find in a scientific journal for geneticists. It has nothing to do with the physical body, disease, illness, or genetic abnormalities. It's a spiritual term that addresses what is lacking in us in a spiritual sense. I first heard the term from a pastor friend of mine several years ago, and it has stuck with me ever since.

My friend would say, "Death is not natural; it is the most unnatural thing in the world, which is why we all hate it." When God created Adam and Eve the intent was that people and God would live eternally with God in a physical paradise. Unfortunately, the consequence of their decision to disobey God unleashed the first unnatural thing into the world, death. When this happened, our spiritual selves were also changed. Our spirits cannot experience physical death because they are not physical. Yet sin corrupts totally, keeping us disconnected from the Jesus.

Thankfully, humanity still possesses the *imago Dei*, or "image of God," in which we were created. Since we are made in the image of God, all people have an innate moral compass that gives us the ability to recognize rudimentary right from wrong. Yet, our broken selves often gravitate toward choosing what is wrong.

Do you remember the first time you told a lie? My guess is your first lie happened after you did something you weren't supposed to. You didn't want to face the consequences, so you lied. Evidence of your spiritually defective DNA is that instead of confessing to whatever you'd done wrong in the first place, you told a lie to cover it up. Have you ever heard the saying "Two wrongs don't make a right?" Our spiritually defective DNA tells us that two wrongs *can* make a right. Or, maybe they won't make the whole situation right, but they might make it right for ourselves. Unfortunately, in the spiritual sense, the situation has only become more wrong.

Knowing we have spiritually defective DNA, Jesus sent the Holy Spirit to us. One function of the Holy Spirit is to convict us of our need for God.

Think of your physical body and the purpose pain serves. In 2013 I ran my first half marathon. For weeks I trained by running five, eight, ten, and finally 13.1 miles. Upon completing my race I felt amazing. It was a real accomplishment. So, the next week I went out running again to keep my body in the shape I had worked so hard to get into. I was two miles in when I felt a small pain in my right knee. The pain was sharp, and increased gradually. It was like a small tear had started and with each step that tear was ripping a little more. The pain told me I had to stop or else things would get worse.

I went to the doctor and learned I had a strain on a ligament. The doctor said that with rest and proper care I could be running again in no time. The pain told me I needed to stop and heal. If I had ignored it, things would only have gotten worse.

Pain is a tool. It alerts us to what has happened. When it comes to our spiritual selves, the feeling we get when we've done wrong does a similar job. It helps to keep us from continuing to participate in harmful behaviors. These feelings, when we listen to them, can prevent major spiritual injuries.

One work of the Holy Spirit is that you feel guilt when you sin. Guilt is the recognition that you did something wrong. (It's not shame, which is the feeling of separation and worthlessness that is accompanied with sin; shame is a powerful tool of the evil one to keep us separated from Jesus.) This type of guilt helps turn your heart and mind to Jesus.

(One note: there is also such a thing as relational guilt. This is not guilt that comes from sin, but guilt produced by our inability, or perceived inability, to meet the expectations of others. This guilt is a product of living in a broken world and not from Jesus.)

Instead of looking for spiritual forgiveness, we often try to solve problems ourselves. We might avoid certain friends for a while, or remove certain apps from our phones, break up with our significant others, or throw tempting things away. Often, we feel an immediate sense of peace because we took action That is, until a few days, weeks, or months later, when we mess up again.

When sin produces guilt in your heart, that guilt is Jesus trying to pull you to himself by helping you see your brokenness. Followers of Jesus don't have to be stuck in the cycle of guilt removal that everyone else is in. You don't have to fix the problem yourself. And as a student leader, you can be an example to your peers of what it looks like to be a follower of Jesus, someone who needs and embraces his forgiveness.

Jesus doesn't expect you to work off your guilt. He allows you to experience it so that you'll recognize that his grace is extended to you. He loves you and forgives you, but he doesn't want you to continue on in your brokenness and sin. Thanks to Jesus's grace, we are connected to God, regardless of our own behavior.

THE PARALYSIS OF SIN

Sin sucks. It messes with our minds, hearts, and souls. It has a way of sneaking into every aspect of our lives. Sin can catch us off guard and wrap itself so tightly around our everyday thoughts, behaviors, desires, and actions that we don't even know it's there, even as we're experiencing its decaying effects. Sin separates and breaks down the closeness between us and God. And yet we sin again and again because we take our spiritually defective DNA with us everywhere we go.

Sometimes we'll recognize our sin, repent, and find freedom. But more often than not we are paralyzed by sin. Day to day we walk around stuck in it. We hear the lies of the enemy:
You aren't good enough to receive the love of God.
Since you already did the wrong thing just keep doing it.
You are worthless, and the world is better off without you.
No one will forgive you for this.
You will always be a disappointment to your parents (or pastor, or friends) because you can't stop this behavior.
It's not so bad; it's actually in your best interest to keep doing what you're doing.

And the lies go on and on.

These untrue words are in direct contrast with what Jesus tells us. Jesus says in John 8:32, "Then you will know the truth, and the truth will set you free." The only way to combat the paralyzing nature of sin is to ground ourselves in the truth of who God says we are. This truth is like a magnetic force that pulls us closer to him.

As a student leader you will often be confronted with lies about who you are because you are serving Jesus on the front lines. When the lies come up and failure happens, don't be paralyzed, but continue moving toward the truth. Below is a list of five common lies you will encounter, and the truth you need to have to overcome these lies and begin moving back toward Jesus.

Lie: I can do it on my own.
This is the trap of thinking you can handle your worries on your own. The truth is that life is hard, and we weren't meant to go it solo. You are not a lone wolf—Christ followers have a squad. This lie is borne out of the shame you may feel at the thought of sharing your issue, or it might come from you telling yourself that your issues are smaller than other people's problems and don't matter to anyone but you.

This lie wants you believe that if you share your struggle you will be judged by others and outcast from the group.

Truth: 1 Peter 5:7. "Cast all your anxiety on him because he cares for you." Everyone has struggles. Sharing them with God and with others will help you move forward. In Jesus and his church you will find people who selflessly want to "carry each other's burdens" (Galatians 6:2). When you get to a point where you think you can or must carry your burdens on your own, then you should make a point to instead invite someone else in.

Lie: I am not qualified.
This lie wants you to believe that because of your sin or past decisions, you can't be used by God. This lie says that God doesn't want you. Extending this thought further, the lie tells you no one else would want you to join in the mission of Jesus, either.

Truth: 1 Peter 2:9. "You are a chosen people, a royal priesthood, a holy nation, God's special possession, that you may declare the praises of him..." When Jesus chose you to be his friend he simultaneously invited you into being on mission with him. He already knows all your weaknesses and he says, "I don't want to do this without you."

Lie: If only I were like [fill in other person's name here].
We tend to look at other people's talents and gifts and wish they were our own. We see what other people can do and compare it to our own abilities. We wrongly think that the best leadership traits are found in others, and believe that we aren't important enough to make a difference.

Truth: 1 Corinthians 12:27. "Now you are the body of Christ, and each one of you is a part of it." Bodies need every part to function well, not just some parts. Did you know that when someone has one toe amputated that person has to relearn how to walk? Most of us would assume someone could lose a toe and be just fine—but ask someone who lost a toe if he would like it back. The answer is yes. The church needs every part to be whole.

Lie: No harm, no foul.

It's easy to believe that our actions are isolated and only affect ourselves, but there is no such thing as an isolated action. Being part of the body of Christ means that every action affects the whole body. Even the small things you do will leave a mark on others.

Truth: Philippians 2:3. "Do nothing out of selfish ambition or vain conceit. Rather, in humility value others above yourselves." When we choose to serve ourselves over others, we are making the wrong choice. We need to be aware of the short-term and long-term effects of our choices before we make them, even if we think they are small and only affect us. Have you ever chosen to not go to youth group because you just didn't want to? Then a friend texts asking if you are going, and you say no. How would your decision influence his decision? Or have you experienced the opposite? You weren't going to go until someone asked if you were. Once you knew the other person was going, you wanted to go too. In many ways our choices affect other people's decisions.

Lie: They can't do it without me.

This is the opposite of feeling disqualified. This lie says that you have the answer, and everyone else is wrong. This lie, one all Christian leaders will face, is the gateway to arrogance.

Truth: Romans 12:3. "Do not think of yourself more highly than you ought, but rather think of yourself with sober judgment, in accordance with the faith God has distributed to each of you." When we see our role in the church through the lens of grace, we realize that no one has more right, privilege, or responsibility than anyone else. This is God's church and ministry, not ours. He has gifted many people to accomplish his mission. Jesus wants you to be a part of it, but not at the exclusion of anyone else.

Lies are complex. They tend to dig their way deep down into our hearts and make us believe ridiculous things about ourselves and other people. In Philippians 4:8 the apostle Paul offers these excellent words, encouraging us to change our focus:

Finally, brothers and sisters, whatever is true, whatever is noble, whatever is right, whatever is pure, whatever is lovely, whatever is admirable—if anything is excellent or praiseworthy—think about such things.

ARROGANCE < HUMILITY (MAINTAIN A TEACHABLE HEART)

Have you ever encountered a know-it-all? These people have something to offer in every scenario. A know-it-all is convinced that his solution is the only solution. Know-it-alls are argumentative and unwilling to consider other opinions. They can be frustrating to work with, and are often manipulative, eager to get what they want and unapologetic when they are wrong. In fact, if accused of being wrong, a know-it-all will find a million ways to justify all his behaviors and probably won't show remorse.

Know-it-alls display arrogance. They have an exaggerated sense of importance. They desperately want to be winners in all things, and often feel discriminated against when things don't go their way.

Commonly, arrogant people have quite a bit of natural talent, and are used to being affirmed for it. The difference between arrogant and humble people is not in their natural talents and spiritual gifts, but in the condition of their hearts. A humble person has a heart that is soft and that recognizes the superiority of God and his kingdom over his or her own desires. Humility is a hard lesson to learn. Proverbs 16:18 says, "Pride goes before destruction, a haughty spirit before a fall." In other words, arrogant people will fall hard, fast, and ugly.

This is the story of King David. He had the skills, the ability, and even the heart that God wanted for a king of Israel. However, years of being king led him into a false sense of superiority. At the height of his arrogance David believed he could have another man's wife for his own, a story that begins in 2 Samuel chapter 11. David managed to convince Bathsheba to have an affair with him while her husband was away at war. When David learned that the affair had produced a pregnancy, he tried to cover it up by having Bathsheba's husband, Uriah the Hittite, come home on leave and sleep with his wife. David's plan was to get Uriah to believe that the child was his. When that didn't work, David had Uriah killed in battle.

No one but David and Bathsheba knew the ins and outs of the affair and what happened to Uriah. David was confident that he had managed to avoid a scandal. But in his arrogance, David forgot that even though no one else knew what happened, God knew. Later, God sent the prophet Nathan to remind David of his sin and of the fact that nothing is hidden from God. When David was confronted he experienced immense guilt and remorse. He repented of his actions, but the damage was already done. God forgave David, but the consequences of his sin with Bathsheba followed the rest of his earthly life. His child with Bathsheba died, his oldest son tried to overthrow David and become king, and he became engaged in warfare with enemies for the rest of his life.

Even after all of this took place, David was considered "a man after [God's] own heart" (1 Samuel 13:14). How is this possible? David was an adulterer and a murderer. But David was willing to repent. Instead of justifying his behavior, he submitted to the lordship of God over his life.

As leaders, this is an important lesson to consider. When you are confronted by others who are upset with your decisions, always start with humility and recognize that it's possible that you are wrong. Then seek to make God-honoring peace—a peace where both sides try to do what is best for Jesus and his mission, not their own personal kingdoms.

When you are motivated to serve Jesus by a desire for him and his kingdom to receive honor and recognition, then you will find yourself serving others with a humble heart. A heart that says, *Regardless of my gain, I can find joy in seeing Jesus gain.* As student leaders it's good to practice the opposite of arrogance: a teachable heart. When you are instructed, listen. When you are confronted, listen. When you are accused, listen. You may find that God is speaking to you through other people. God used Nathan to help David understand his own actions and seek God. Is there someone like Nathan in your life?

ARE YOU A LEADER?

What and who has God entrusted into your care? Throughout the Bible, we see a number of men and women who had little to no influence in their communities, and yet were chosen by God for important things. Gideon is one of my favorite examples. Gideon had no obvious qualities of leadership, but God chose to entrust him with significant influence. Even Gideon thought it was crazy for God to choose him. Listen to his objections when God asks him to serve in Judges 6:15: "'Pardon me, my lord,' Gideon replied, 'but how can I save Israel? My clan is the weakest in Manasseh, and I am the least in my family.'" God used the lowest ranking member of the lowest ranking tribe to lead a nation into war, one that would eventually bring freedom from oppression to the nation of Israel. God trusted Gideon, and Gideon used that trust as God intended, to bring about social reformation and move people into deeper friendship with himself.

You might be entrusted with a lot, or with very little. What matters is that you use what you're trusted with to serve Jesus.

One of my close friends, Glen, is a true leader. He spends his life working to ensure the gifts, talents, and skills of the people God has entrusted into his care are being used to advance the mission of Jesus. When you spend time with Glen the conversation is never about Glen and what he is doing or how much he has accomplished (although as the overseer of the international mission strategy of a large church in Pittsburgh his responsibility is significant). Instead, the focus is entirely on you. He has a way of making you feel like you are the only person in the room and that his primary concerns are your heart, soul, and well-being. A few years ago as I was talking with Glen he shared how humbled he feels to "walk among giants in the faith." When I looked at Glen I realized that the reason he was "walking among giants" is that he had spent his life lifting others up to their spiritual heights.

Glen has been entrusted by God with the spiritual formation of many people. However brief a time he has with another person, he sees his chief role as bringing to the forefront the best of the gifts God has entrusted that person with. Glen has been a major spiritual influence for countless people, and without him, thousands of people would never have become friends with Jesus.

When we take seriously the care of the things and people God has entrusted us with, we begin to participate in real spiritual leadership. The life of Jesus was characterized not by the influence he sought to accumulate for himself, but by the empowerment of the people he chose to surround himself with.

In my opinion, the greatest statement of leadership Jesus ever uttered is Mark 10:45: "For even the Son of Man did not come to be served, but to serve, and to give his life as a ransom for many." His greatest desire is to unleash the positive things he instilled in you when you were created. Jesus wants to lift you up and entrust you with more. With whatever you've been entrusted, God has asked you to serve in a way that moves people deeper into friendship with Jesus.

Think about what and who God has placed in your care. When you start with a desire to care, serve, and bring out the best in others, you, like my friend Glen, get to change the world for Jesus.

YOU AREN'T THE JUDGE
On August 28, 1963, Dr. Martin Luther King Jr. delivered his famous "I Have a Dream" speech. You likely remember one of its most powerful lines: "I have a dream that my four little children will one day live in a nation where they will not be judged by the color of their skin, but by the content of their character."[4] Dr. King understood well humanity's tendency to discount people for reasons that are unfounded, unjust, and often evil.

The divisive judgement of others is not always as blatant as it is in the case of racism. We all have a tendency to judge. This is a survival instinct that is rooted in our spiritually defective DNA. Its sole purpose is to place ourselves in a position of superiority over other people. This type of judgement caries the implications that other people are less than. Consciously and unconsciously we carry around this judgement filter, which has damaging implications on our effectiveness as leaders and Christ followers.

In John 3:30, John the Baptist says of Jesus, "He must become greater; I must become less." John the Baptist had a highly influential ministry. He had followers traveling from all over the ancient world to listen to his teaching. Shortly after John's ministry began, Jesus began his ministry as well. These two men, who happened to be cousins, were both starting to gain a following. John, in his wisdom and humility, recognized the ministry of Jesus as greater than his own. Instead of jockeying for spiritual influence, John willingly stepped into the background and allowed Jesus to take center stage.

John was a leader God trusted with a very specific ministry. He cared well for what God trusted him with, and ensured that in all things Jesus would be glorified, even if it meant he had less influence of his own. Too often, leaders place themselves in a positive light to the detriment of others. There is often real temptation to put others down, whether publicly or privately, especially when we see it will directly benefit us.

When these temptations and opportunities arise it helps to spend time thinking about our friendship with Jesus. Jesus knows everything about us, good and bad. And yet he sought, at great expense to himself, to lift us up, honor us, and bring us back into unity with God. We should act as Jesus did, allowing no space in our hearts to think of ourselves as superior to anyone. We may possess different talents, levels of popularity, and degrees of influence, but we are equally loved and valued by God. Great leaders recognize this truth and live into the old adage, "treat everyone as you would like to be treated." If Jesus was willing to be your friend despite your positives and negatives, then, as far as it is up to you, do the same.

Reflection Questions: Know Your Humanity

1. Dan (this book's author) uses the term "DNA." What is one positive trait you inherited from your parents?

2. What does God's grace mean to you as someone who has spiritually defective DNA? How can we show God thankfulness for his grace, even though we may experience the same patterns of brokenness repeatedly in our life?

3. Go through each of the lies mentioned in the chapter and, as a group but without naming names, come up with examples of how you've seen these lies in real life:

   • I can do it on my own
   • I'm not qualified
   • If only I were like [fill in other person's name here]
   • No harm, no foul
   • They can't do it without me

4. Which of the lies described resonates with you? (That is, which one tends to be sometimes true of you?)

   • I can do it on my own
   • I'm not qualified
   • If only I were like [fill in other person's name here]
   • No harm, no foul
   • They can't do it without me

5. Of all the things covered in this chapter, what was most meaningful for you and why?

The Awesomeness of Relationship
Student leaders are growing as ones who embrace well.

Who is in your squad? (Or posse, gang, team, group, text thread, group chat, or however you define your crew.) What people do you tend to connect with the most? In the study of behavioral sciences, the word used to describe the groups we find ourselves in is *tribe*.

Tribes are not new concepts. Since the foundations of human society, people have been branching ourselves off into groups of others with shared values, attitudes, and behaviors. This helped with our physical preservation, but it was also helpful emotionally. When we meet people similar to us and find a measure of loyalty in them, we begin to form our tribe.

To belong in a tribe, you must behave, believe, and participate in its practices. For the original members of the tribe these practices develop naturally. However, as new people are introduced to the tribe, the tribe clarifies the rules for belonging. We've all seen examples. Churches create membership documents, sports teams create contracts, and best friend groups may even create pacts. In our deep desire to belong we conform to these expectations. We find ourselves adjusting our beliefs, attitudes, and values to receive a communal connection.

As a Christ follower you now belong to a new tribe, a spiritual tribe in which you can find unity with all other believers. I never fully understood this until I traveled to Spain on a mission trip. I was sitting on the beach in Barcelona with Spanish Christians. We didn't share the same language, but we shared the same faith, values, and practices. On that beach we worshiped together, speaking different languages but a unified tribe. But you don't have to go to Spain to understand this concept. Try attending a few different churches in your community. You will quickly see that while the culture feels somewhat different, they are each part of the same tribe.

The church is a tribe of many tribes, with one chief whose name is Jesus. Within the greater tribe there are written expectations found in the Bible for all followers of Jesus, but there are unwritten ones locally. This localized tribe creates its own culture, values, and behaviors. At some point, if you participate in a local church or ministry, you'll be expected to follow suit. There is not a church in the world that, after you've attended for a few months, won't ask you to serve personally or give financially. If you want to enjoy the full status of belonging, there will be expectations placed on you.

This book won't address local expectations for belonging, but rather kingdom expectations. What does it mean to truly belong to the tribe known as Christians? More importantly, what does Jesus expect of you as a tribe member, and how can you experience the unity of the Holy Spirit with all believers?

4 Own Your Gifts and Priorities

KNOWING YOUR SPIRITUAL GIFTS

When you joined the Jesus tribe you were given a very specific set of gifts. 1 Corinthians 12:11 (NLT) says, "It is the one and only Spirit who distributes all these gifts. He alone decides which gift each person should have." These gifts were given to you with joy and intentionality. Only you, using these gifts in your context, can bring about the spiritual changes Jesus wants in your community. You have an important role to play, and when you play it you will experience a deep sense of belonging.

There are several ways to determine which spiritual gifts you were given. I recommend a spiritual gifts assessment tool found at www.spiritualgiftstest.com. At the time of this writing they offer a free online test that will indicate what gifts you might possess, as well as a personality assessment.

I once took a spiritual gifts assessment, a test that asked 100 different questions about things I did or didn't like. I later realized, though, that the questions were evaluating my preferences, not determining my actual gifts. One question related to the spiritual gift of healing: "Do you find yourself fascinated by medical trauma or repulsed?" At the time I had an infected ingrown toenail. Daily I was digging at my toe, trying to remove the infection. I thought it was cool. It was the same type of gross fascination that leads people into a YouTube spiral of videos of cyst or blackhead removal.

There were several similar questions, and in the end I scored high for the gift of healing. However, this new "gift" in the hands of a seventeen-year-old made for some interesting trial and error. Let's just say, my friend Jared still has a prosthetic leg. I didn't have this gift, I just had a fascination with the body and medical things.

I later learned that the spiritual gift of healing is not about a propensity to learn medicine or a fascination with infections. It is about allowing the Holy Spirit of God to perform miraculous healing. It is literally the same work of healing Jesus did in the New Testament, enabling the lame to walk and the blind to see. A spiritual gifts assessment is a great way to start determining your potential gifts, but isn't the stopping point. Below is a three-part process to learn what your gifts are.

Affinity
You will feel an affinity—a natural liking or sense of attraction—for your spiritual gifts, and you will love using them. You might get a sense of what your gifts are by watching others. If you have the gift of teaching, you might see a teacher and say, "I would love to do that someday." If you read about spiritual gifts you will likely find yourself drawn to some more than others. Taking a spiritual gifts assessment can help you think through what spiritual gifts you are drawn to.

Use It and Look for Affirmation
Discipling relationships help us determine how to use our spiritual gifts. We all need leaders and mentors, people who can call out and affirm what is already inside of us. Around the time I took a spiritual gifts assessment I had my spiritual leaders affirm the giftings in my life. They could see what I couldn't see about myself. If you have an affinity for a gift and other people affirm it, then it's time to start trying it out. In Romans 12:6 Paul says, "We have different gifts, according to the grace given to each of us. If your gift is

prophesying, then prophesy in accordance with your faith." Simply put, if you feel you have it, then just try it! If you think you have the gift of teaching then teach about the Bible and see if it changes hearts and minds. If you have the gift of helps, then help others, expecting God to use your helping to change hearts.

After using a gift, see if others can affirm that Jesus used you in a meaningful way. In the spiritual world using gifts should encourage the body of the believers and help people move closer to Jesus. If you can see those two things happening when you use a gift, then you are the right track.

Opportunity

Ephesians 2:10 says, "For we are God's handiwork, created in Christ Jesus to do good works, which God prepared in advance for us to do." The good works referred to in this verse are not just good deeds. They are works of a spiritual nature that transform the landscape of the spiritual world. When we use our gifts, it helps to transform and heal the world, and will always honor Jesus. These opportunities are around us every day. We don't have to be at church or on a mission trip to use our spiritual gifts. Your gifts and mine are meant to be used in every part of our world, in every part of our lives. Using these gifts leads to a greater sense of purpose and belonging in Jesus's tribe. It's also just a lot more fun than not. We are spirit-filled believers, and we can use our spiritual gifts to the fullest.

The chart below lists some verses that describe spiritual gifts. Read through them and think about what you feel an affinity for. Talk with a trusted leader about what he or she sees in you. Consider taking a spiritual gifts assessment and reading more on this topic to learn about how to discover and use the gifts God has given you.

Romans 12:6–8	1 Corinthians 12:8–10	1 Peter 4:11
Prophecy, Serving, Teaching, Exhortation, Giving, Leadership, Mercy	Wisdom, Knowledge, Faith, Healing, Miracles, Prophesy, Distiguishing Between Spirits, Tongues, Interpretation of Tongues.	Speaking Helping

PRIORITY #1: THE CHURCH

The church was established by Jesus in his last days on earth before the ascension. Although we often think of church as a building, Jesus did not build a brick and mortar structure, call it "the church," and then fly up to God. The earliest Christians didn't even have a place outside of homes to gather together. The church is simply a group of people who are sharing in the mission of Jesus. The word used in the Greek is *ekklesia*, which basically translates to "a group of faithful people." This is why Jesus says in Matthew 18:20, "For where two or three gather in my name, there am I with them." If you are with followers of Jesus, you are the church.

People have always been and will always be God's plan for reaching the world. After all, we humans are the most advanced communication technology ever created. We are storytellers by nature and we create beautiful ways of sharing information. Since the gospel literally means "good news," the best option Jesus had for getting his message into the world was to start a movement of friends who had a deep and satisfying relationship with him.

Early followers of Jesus weren't known as Christians, and weren't identified with buildings and meeting places. They were called followers of "The Way" (Acts 9:2). These followers of The Way were people who knew or had heard of Jesus and were living according to his teachings. They got this name because of Jesus's well-known proclamation in John 14:6, "I am the way and the truth and the life. No one comes to the Father except through me." Jesus's followers were recognized not for their location, but because of how they lived. When all the followers of Jesus were together, the Holy Spirit showed up with them. In Acts 2, the Holy Spirit gave this gathering of followers of The Way the ability to speak in different languages, allowing them to invite people outside of their group into friendship with Jesus.

The church is not a Sunday morning experience, but a daily experience. As a student leader, one of your top priorities should be intentionally and often spending time with other followers of The Way. This might mean prioritizing church events, and spending time with good friends, your family, or a leader or mentor. When you spend time with other followers of The Way, you are creating room for the Holy Spirit to show you how to participate in the mission of Jesus, inside and outside of a church building.

As you build relationships with other followers of The Way, remember that the mission of the church is to help all people become friends with Jesus, not just the people in your inner circle. Jesus isn't exclusive in his friendship, and he doesn't want us to be either. He offers friendship to everyone who wants it, and he wants his friends to be friends with each other, inviting others in.

PRIORITY #2: ACCOMPLISHING THE GOOD WORKS SET ASIDE FOR YOU

Too often we make serving Jesus about us. But there is nothing that will earn us more or less friendship with Jesus. Any sense of performance-driven pressure is not from Jesus. We tend to make discipleship about living a certain way and doing the right things, rather than about being friends with the God who transforms us. We can never fully separate ourselves from our brokenness. When we miss the mark, we may even tell ourselves that Jesus is disappointed in us. This kind of thinking has to stop. Jesus cares far less about you behaving a certain way than about you having a relationship with him and allowing that relationship to transform your life.

As imperfect people we cannot hope to engage in the mission of Jesus perfectly. Jesus says the greatest commandment is to "love the Lord your God with all your heart and with all your soul and with all your mind" (Matthew 22:37). Secondly, he says to "love your neighbor as yourself. All the Law and the Prophets hang on these two commandments" (Matthew 22:39).

There's something encouraging to note here: these two expectations are all about the heart, *not* about behavior. We will never do things perfectly, but if we focus on acting out of love for God and love for others, we can step confidently into the good works Jesus has set aside for us.

Jesus shares important words in Matthew 25:40: "The King will reply, 'Truly I tell you, whatever you did for one of the least of these brothers and sisters of mine, you did for me.'" Reflect on those words. Are you thinking about pursuing justice for the disenfranchised, creating spaces where everyone belongs, finding homes for the orphans, and caring for the motherless and widows? Following Jesus is about serving one another in love, not about monitoring one another's behavior.

Jesus's mission is to bring grace to everyone, not condemnation. He wants us to help relieve both the physical and spiritual sufferings of the people who aren't yet friends with him, and continue to do even more for those who already are. The apostle Paul encourages us to "carry each other's burdens." In this way we are loving God with all our heart, soul, and mind, and loving our neighbor as ourselves.

I believe the gospel of Jesus has the power to transform hearts, which is the ultimate miracle. And yet, we can never separate that from the call of Jesus to meet people's tangible, practical needs. The truth is that we are best able to experience the grace of God when we are extending all the grace we can to others.

PRIORITY #3: BEING A LOVING SERVANT

Being a student leader means putting the interests of others above your own. Ask yourself a few questions: Do you put others before yourself? At school? At home? At work? On vacation? If not, why? Often the answer is simple: time. It goes against the fabric of our flesh to spend time, the single nonrenewable resource we have, doing things we don't want to. Student leadership means spending time working for the good of other people. It's impossible to avoid resentment unless it is done out of love.

A few months ago I was asked to speak at a middle school and high school camp weekend. Most speakers have a speaking and expense fee for their services. It is not much compensation, but enough to make you feel like your time is valued. After I verbally agreed to the weekend, I was informed they had no money to pay for my services and could only cover my travel expenses. This is not what I was expecting. I want to tell you that I didn't care if I got paid. After all,

I am servant leader. But I did. I was immediately deflated. This was going to be a lot of work and cost me more than one weekend's worth of time. It would mean days of preparation, study, and writing. Not to mention it would cost me personal time. Feeling upset, I told the organizers that before I could commit, I needed to go home and consult with my wife to make sure it was okay to take the time away from family.

The truth is that I was trying to find a way to graciously back out of this opportunity. (I'm guessing you might be able to relate. Have you ever said you needed to check with your parents before saying yes to something, when really you were just trying to find a way out of an obligation? And maybe you never even asked them? Most of us have been there.) I was hoping my family would say I shouldn't do the weekend speaking engagement, and with that excuse available I wouldn't look like an unreasonable, selfish jerk when I called back to decline the offer.

I spoke with my wife that night. She looked me in the eyes and said, "I won't say no for you. You have to determine if this is what the Lord is asking you to do, regardless of money." She was urging me to reflect: could I serve without expectation? Did I love the people God was calling me to serve more than a few hundred dollars?

I walked away frustrated that she wouldn't say no for me, even though I knew this was an unfair position to place her in. The next morning I planned to call the camp organizers and say no. Then, as I was reading the Bible, I came across a passage that made me rethink things: "Each of you should use whatever gift you have received to serve others, as faithful stewards of God's grace in its various forms" (1 Peter 4:10). I realized that I was refusing to use my gifts to extend God's grace to others because I wasn't being given any immediate return. Convicted, I called the camp and agreed to come. After all, the kingdom of Jesus is about Jesus, not about me.

I ended up having an amazing weekend. A half dozen teenagers said yes to being friends with Jesus for the first time. A fourteen-year-old guy named Derrick really connected with the content, and we spent significant time talking through healing he needed to experience from his parents' divorce, and his unhealthy relationship with his significant other. God used that weekend to move people closer to himself, and I would have missed out on all of that if I had stayed home because of money.

Are there times when it is okay to say no when you are asked to serve? Yes. But when you say no because you value yourself over others, you are acting selfishly, and not as a loving servant. Galatians 6:10 says, "Therefore, as we have opportunity, let us do good to all people, especially to those who belong to the family of believers." In other words, if it is not at the expense of your own or someone else's spiritual, emotional, or physical well-being, serving is always the right choice. When you serve others, God will honor it. As Hebrews 6:10 says, "God is not unjust; he will not forget your work and the love you have shown him as you have helped his people and continue to help them."

PRIORITY #4: REACHING OUT

When I was seventeen years old a mentor gave me a mantra I have repeated ever since: "It's not about me. It's all about Jesus! Therefore, I will lead the way." At first, this seems like a contradictory statement. But what she explained to me is that when the mission of Jesus is our priority, we should always be seeking out opportunities to participate in it. We don't do this because we want glory or to be noticed. We do it because the mission of Jesus is too important to do nothing. Doing nothing is a choice, and usually a choice based in fear of failure.

There is a phrase attributed to hockey legend Wayne Gretzky: "You miss one hundred percent of the shots you don't take." Wayne Gretzky didn't become one of the greatest hockey players of all time because he skated fast, had great puck handling skills, or could hold his own in a hockey fight. All of that was part of it, of course, but he was one of the best because he wasn't afraid to take every shot he had—even if he missed. When Gretzky retired in 1999 he had taken 5,088 shots and scored 894 times. That is a 17.6 percent success rate. (To put it another way, he missed 82.4 percent of the time). And it made him the highest-scoring hockey player of all time.[5]

Jesus gave you gifts, talents, skills, and dreams. Sometimes you may be too scared to even verbalize these dreams, let alone pursue them. But, if the dreams come from God, then you would do well to pursue them, even if you miss and things don't turn out the way you hope. Sometimes the good works Jesus has set apart for you to do will become opportunities—if you chase the dreams God has placed in your heart.

In Numbers 13:1-33, God is leading the Israelites into the land he promised to Abraham 400 years earlier (a story that's in Genesis 15). Israel sent twelve spies into the land to determine if they had the strength, skills, and resources available to enter successfully. They wanted to know they could fulfill the promise God had made to Abraham: that they would gain the land and secure victory over the current inhabitants. The twelve spies returned, reporting that there were giant Philistines and many obstacles to overcome. In fear, they complained to Moses and decided they didn't want the promised land after all. They were too afraid to take a chance.

Seeing their fear and lack of faith, the Lord sent the Israelites to wander the desert for forty years until their hearts were ready to follow him. Over those forty years the nation of Israel dreamed of what it would be like to finally leave the desert and inhabit the promised land. What would have happened, though, if they would have decided to follow their dreams the first time, rather than give in to their fear?

When there is a dream bubbling in your heart or an opportunity to do something for Jesus that seems unattainable by your own effort, you are in the perfect spot to reach out and take the shot. You aren't shooting blindly. You are going in faith that the Lord is with you. In these moments you can have confidence that God will honor your decision to do something for him. You may only be successful 17.6 percent of the time, but that's okay. It could make all the difference in someone else's world. It's not about you—it's all about Jesus. Therefore, you can lead the way.

Reflection Questions: Own Your Gifts and Priorities

1. It's pretty clear from the New Testament that the church is God's "Plan A" for discipleship and outreach. Name a couple of things you have come to really appreciate about your church.

2. God gives people different gifts to use in ministry. As you think about your church or youth leaders, name some of the people and the strengths and gifts you have observed in them.

3. Looking over the list of spiritual gifts provided, what is one gift you think you have? What is one gift you have questions about?

4. Being a student leader implies you are both "a loving servant" and someone who is "reaching out." Your spiritual gifts influence which of these comes most naturally to you. Discuss your role as a student leader and what being a "loving servant" and "reaching out" look like in your youth group.

5 Own Your Relationships with People

BE THE FIRST TO SHOW GRACE

Serving with others is a lot like brushing long hair. You can brush the knots out in the morning, but they come back by night. As the father of four girls I feel like I have spent countless hours brushing hair. It doesn't matter how often you brush or the products you use; the hair is destined to knot back up. Getting out knots is painful. The brush doesn't remove knots effortlessly. It pulls, stretches, and often even breaks the hair in the process. This is why brushes are filled with those strands of hair that make them look gross to anyone but their owner. Those strands in the brush were knotted and resistant, and were removed by force.

As we serve others there will be times when it is easy, beautiful, and wonderful. But sooner or later, we will encounter some kind of knot, one that will need to be untangled before it contributes to a bigger knot that's even harder to remove. It may be drama between best friends, people failing to follow through on their responsibilities, gossip, or anything else that happens because people aren't perfect and mess up often.

When we're in a conflict with someone else, it's easy to feel prideful. It's easy to expect the other person to come and apologize first, rather than be the one to apologize. However, in any given conflict there is rarely only one person to blame.

Imagine you come across a log in the woods that you decide to bring home. This log is too big to carry alone, so you recruit someone to help you. You assure her it will only take ten minutes.

At first, you both feel energetic and are mutually carrying the weight. Over time, though, one of you will become more tired than the other. It might be a strength or a stamina issue, but sooner or later one person ends up carrying more weight. Let's say the friend you recruited is now carrying seventy percent of the weight, and you are carrying thirty percent. It's a bigger job than you anticipated. Your ten-minute task has become a thirty-minute ordeal.

In your emotional distress you decide to apologize for the work being harder and taking longer than you estimated. You intuitively know an apology, even for a slight frustration, will do wonders in keeping harmony between you. Your small act of seeking forgiveness will not only ease your friend's emotional frustration, but can strengthen your friendship. When you seek forgiveness, you invite grace into the relationship. You're letting the other person know you respect her work and time. Seeking forgiveness also expresses your deep-felt gratitude for your friend's service. The simple act of apologizing first creates space for grace to abound.

A friend always invites grace into conflicts and knots when they are small. There is much less hurt, pain, and frustration this way. Jesus says in Matthew 5:23-24,

> "So if you are offering your gift at the altar and there remember that your brother has something against you, leave your gift there before the altar and go. First be reconciled to your brother, and then come and offer your gift."

In other words, the impetus is on you to seek forgiveness for whatever you did. This principle is not only true when you are on the thirty percent side of the log, but also when you're on the seventy percent side.

And what if you are the one being asked for forgiveness? In that case, you are the one in a position of emotional power. You may feel indignant and used, but keep in mind that the attitude you show your friend will have a lasting impact on her emotional state and your future friendship. Being in this position of power requires you to exercise more grace than the person who was mistaken. A negative response from you very well may tip the emotional scales, and could cause permanent divisiveness. Before you know it, carrying that log could become one of the forty things you are holding against one another. If pride keeps you from offering grace, the small knot may become a rat's nest.

You may be wondering, who is more responsible? The person who makes the initial mistake and asks forgiveness, or the person who fails to show forgiveness? The answer is easy: the one who doesn't forgive. When you hold the emotional power, you are the one more responsible for ensuring that grace prevails between you.

This is why Jesus instructs us in Matthew 18:15 (NLT), "If another believer sins against you, go privately and point out the offense. If the other person listens and confesses it, you have won that person back." When you are wronged and choose to invite grace into the relationship, you are providing space for forgiveness to reign supreme. Healthy leaders constantly seek forgiveness—and provide it without being asked. They understand the depth of their own forgiveness by Jesus. They recognize their own imperfections. They see the value of getting out knots while they are small to avoid the big knots later.

SEEK OPPORTUNITIES TO LIFT OTHERS UP

There will come times when it seems impossible to keep going. I once went through a single week where my girlfriend broke up with me at a Dunkin' Donuts, I was placed on the waiting list for the college I wanted to attend, and I had to spend a few hundred dollars to get my truck fixed. It was like a bad country song written about a seventeen-year-old kid. Life has a way of bombarding you with one thing after the next: anxiety over your future career, boyfriend and girlfriend issues, conflict between your parents, conflict with your friends, failure and disappointment when taking exams or trying out for a team, not being able to get the concert ticket you want, forgetting lines of the play you are in… As Jesus says in John 16:33, "In this world you will have trouble." Thanks, Jesus, for stating the obvious. But Jesus loves us more than to drop the mic and walk away with that pithy phrase. He continues by declaring, "But take heart! I have overcome the world."

This promise is a gift to every friend of Jesus. It reminds us of the truth that in all things Jesus is still in control. When we keep this perspective it breeds within us a deep faith—faith meaning the confidence that our hopes will come to pass. Jesus is the one who will sustain us and help us overcome any troubles we encounter.

Jesus is the one who overcomes, and he invites us to participate in the ministry of comfort with him. Since Jesus is not physically present on earth, he asks his people to stand in his place and be his hands and feet. He declares that we should love one another. Recall what it says in Galatians 6:2: "Carry each other's burdens, and in this way you will fulfill the law of Christ." There are times when we need show sacrificial love to those around us. There are also times when we need to reach out and ask for help.

In Exodus 17 there is a story about the Israelites' first battle during their time in the wilderness. Moses climbs to the top of a hill and looks down upon the battle scene. As the fighting rages he lifts his hands in prayer. As his hands are raised the Israelites begin to win. Moses, being a man in his eighties, quickly wears out, and his hands begin to drop. As his hands drop, the battle begins to shift and the Israelites start to lose. Aaron, Moses's brother, sees what is happening and recruits a man name Hur. Aaron and Hur stand on either side of Moses, lifting his hands into the air until the battle is over and the Israelites see victory. Without Aaron stepping in—which he does without being asked—the battle would have been lost.

This is an example of carrying someone else's burden. All of us are walking through some kind of trouble. Other followers of Jesus have been placed in our lives to lift up our hands for us. Because we live in a highly independent culture, the concept of asking for help is almost foreign. It can seem belittling to admit weakness and let others know you need help. Thankfully, as followers of Jesus we aren't told to wait to help until someone asks. Instead, we are instructed to step in before that person asks and see him or her through.

When you are in a relationship there will come times when you need the other person to lift up your hands. There will also be times when you'll have the opportunity to lift up the other person's hands. Good leaders always take the time to lift up the hands of those around them. They step in without being asked and model the way we should treat each other. As a student leader, modeling this gives other people unspoken permission to step into your life during your times of trouble and become the ones who help you through.

Who in your life is currently in need of your help? Who can you stand with as they walk through troubles? Jesus says, "By this everyone will know that you are my disciples, if you love one another" (John 13:35). Your act of lifting someone up actually lifts up the name of Jesus and makes you that much more of a participant in the mission of Jesus.

BUILD TRUTH-FILLED RELATIONSHIPS

There is quote from the movie *A Few Good Men*. In the movie, Jack Nicholson's character has taken the witness stand in the court of law and is being repeatedly asked to tell the truth. He responds with a classic line: "You want answers? You can't handle the truth!" In the story, Nicholson's character is protecting a lie. He believes that telling people what really happened would do more harm than good.[6]

Many of us live like this in our day-to-day relationships. We omit the whole truth, or even flat out lie, because we believe it is better for everyone. (Or if we're being honest, we probably just think it's better for ourselves.) Sometimes, we believe that the truth might make others disappointed in us or cause greater conflict. We fear that if people found out the real details they would think less of us.

Because it's easier, our tendency is to omit the truth or lie to protect ourselves. We also tend to avoid speaking truth into other people's lives. To speak truth sometimes means to call out a lie that someone else believes or is telling. Speaking the truth is important—but it's also risky. I have often seen issues with this arise between friends. One friend observes that another friend is, for example, treating his parents badly, or in a toxic relationship. Because the friend who notices this behavior wants the other person to be happy and doesn't want to hurt the friendship, he bites his tongue, and the damaging behaviors continue until they grow far worse. Or there will be dangerous choices, like teen drinking or drinking and driving. Instead of speaking up, a concerned friend may say nothing. This avoids conflict in the moment, but far greater trouble is likely coming.

The apostle Paul says, "…speaking the truth in love, we will grow to become in every respect the mature body of him who is the head, that is, Christ" (Ephesians 4:15). If we are going to be mature followers of Jesus, we need to become people comfortable with speaking the truth to others, and comfortable with inviting them to do the same for us. In our friendship with Jesus the primary characteristic is his grace bestowed upon us. We are asked to show the same grace to others in all circumstances. When grace abounds, so does truth. When both grace and truth are present, trust also grows.

The greater the trust you have with someone, the easier truth-filled relationships are. This is why dishonesty in our closest relationships hurts so deeply. When we recognize that we've been lied to, either overtly or by omission, we may feel like the relationship was devalued: the other person didn't trust you enough to share the truth with you.

A few months ago, I was struck by a verse: "Therefore confess your sins to each other and pray for each other so that you may be healed" (James 5:16). At the time, I had been keeping something secret from my best friend, my wife. I was certain that if I told her this secret, it would ruin our relationship. In my desire to protect what was good, I was actually creating a division between us. My lack of confession was sickening our relationship.

After reading this verse, I took the difficult step of sharing my secret with my wife and bringing truth into our relationship. Her response blew me away. I was anticipating that more brokenness would come from my confession, but instead I found healing and renewal. Our relationship became stronger, closer, and healthier. It did not remove some of the consequences of my secret, but the grace that flowed with the sharing of the truth allowed us to navigate what had happened in a restorative way.

Before I confessed my secret to my wife I had been feeling trapped. I was imprisoned in my lie, and the walls of that prison perpetuated a division between us. When I confessed, I was set free from the prison I had built with my own hands. Is it any wonder that Jesus says in John 8:32, "Then you will know the truth, and the truth will set you free"? There is spiritual power in the truth because it invites the grace of Jesus into our relationships.

Who have you have been keeping the truth from? Where have unhealthy secrets been kept? Who do you need to speak with, clearing the air so that the pleasing aroma of grace can arise? Truth-filled relationships are powerful and God-honoring. Trust the promise of God that healing comes from confession, and that the truth will set you free.

SUBMIT TO THE RIGHT AUTHORITIES

I love being a decision maker. It brings me great joy to have control over situations and outcomes. There is nothing more thrilling than to make big decisions that have real impact on many people's lives, including my own.

Decisions carry with them unintended consequences. For example, when you choose to go to college, the financial consideration is immense. If you have to take out loans, those loans will become not just your burden, but the burden of your future spouse. If your parents are assisting with payments, then your decision has real financial consequences for their bank account. While the decision is yours to make, it has impact that extends far beyond you.

BECOMING A STUDENT LEADER

As a teenager I was attending a youth conference at the University of Wisconsin. Late in the afternoon a massive storm rolled through the area, causing flooding and significant hail damage. Cars were under three to four feet of water in low-lying places. As the water receded, several hundred teenagers, including myself, began to turn the lawn into a giant muddy slip and slide. While there was already some damage to the lawn because of the flooding, our actions contributed significantly more harm the property.

A few minutes into this, an adult came out and began chastising us. Right away, thirty to forty of the teenagers present—embarrassingly, myself included (okay, I *may* have been the one who started the whole thing…), began chanting at this adult, "GO A-WAY." Shortly after that our youth pastors showed up and started grabbing teenagers and hauling us away. The next morning, we learned that the slip and slide caused several thousand dollars in damages. Our actions had significant consequences and left the university staff with a huge mess to clean up.

When we were told to stop by the adult, our hearts were in rebellion mode. We wanted to keep doing what we wanted to do. Several people suffered the consequences of their actions by being sent home early. Fortunately, I wasn't one of them, but I should have been. What would have been the response if we had simply listened to this adult, respected that person's authority, and stopped? I guarantee no one would have been sent home at all.

Submitting to another person's authority can be difficult, but people in authority are there for a good reason. They have wisdom, experience, and perspective, and are responsible for seeing the whole picture, while the rest of us may only see the small part that affects ourselves. Though sometimes authority figures carry out injustice— they are as human and flawed as the rest of us—the role of authority is incredibly important.

The apostle Paul says in Romans 13:1, "Let everyone be subject to the governing authorities…The authorities that exist have been established by God." What are some authorities in your life that you don't want to submit to? Why is that? What could be the benefit of submitting to their instruction?

Reflection Questions: Own Your Relationships with People

1. Give everyone paper, a pencil or pen, and a hard surface to draw on. On your paper, draw a picture of a conflict situation, or something that represents what conflict feels like to you. When everyone is finished, take turns explaining your pictures.

2. Can you think of a time when you did something wrong and the person you wronged gave you grace instead of punishment? If so, explain.

3. In your own life, which comes easier: being the first to show grace, or lifting people up? Why do you think that is?

4. In your youth group, if you, as student leaders, got better at showing grace and lifting people up, what would be the impact? Another way to think of it: when new people come for the first time, what would they feel? What would they notice?

5. Practically speaking, what do you think it means to build truth-filled relationships? Also, why is it especially important for the relationships and interactions in our leadership team to be truth-filled?

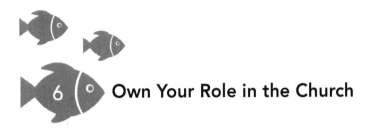

6 Own Your Role in the Church

BECOME AN INVITER

The church is a group of people who gather together voluntarily. This is one of the joys of being a Christian, and we do it to worship God, experience community, and enjoy one another's company. In our culture, Christians have the opportunity to regularly be in relationship with others who are also friends with Jesus. The beautiful thing is that this community we call church is for everyone.

For many of your friends, "going to church" is probably a foreign concept. A church is a community of people they don't know and a set of practices they aren't familiar with. I often use the phrase, "If it's not normal it's weird." When someone is invited to church for the first time it can be weird, but that's okay. The goal of inviting people to church is to give them an opportunity to have an encounter with Jesus and become part of a fully accepting community.

At my church we have a core value, "come as you are." This represents the beauty of Jesus's grace. He wants all people to come as they are and experience who he is. No one needs to dress, talk, or behave a certain way, and we shouldn't expect anyone to. That would be weird. Again, the goal of inviting someone into your community is for that person to be welcomed into an environment where he or she might have a meaningful encounter with Jesus. If we truly believe that friendship with Jesus is the best thing that could ever happen to someone, we need to be intentional about inviting people into community with other followers of Jesus.

Sometimes, it's scary to invite others to share in a faith community with us. We worry they might see something in us they haven't before. But you are simply inviting your friends to be part of another area of your life, and bringing your faith into the conversation.

Helping people encounter Jesus is rarely an individual effort. This is why the apostle Paul encourages us to be the hand or foot of Jesus (1 Corinthians 12:15). You really can't be both the hands and the feet. You are just one friend of Jesus. It takes multiple believers in relationship with someone who doesn't know Jesus for that person to encounter the fullness of God. This is why inviting someone into your faith community is so important. Together, the body of believers can help that person develop an understanding of personal friendship with Jesus.

When I was in high school I was invited to attend a rival school's basketball game. I didn't know the people or the fans, but I understood basketball. I wouldn't have gone to the game on my own, but my friends cared about the team, and I wanted to belong with this group, so I began to do what they did. After going to multiple games with the same people I started to become personally invested in the team. Before I knew it, I was a fan. I wanted to go to the games even when my friends weren't going.

When you are an inviter, it shows that you want your friends to be part of your life, especially the most meaningful, powerful, and transformative aspects. Inviting someone to be part of your community of faith usually makes that person feel loved, appreciated, and connected to you in a deeper way than before. Your friends may find the practices of the faith community a bit weird, but they'll probably tolerate the weird because they genuinely like you. Many of us have friends we would love to invite to church, but don't because we fear that they might reject us. The truth is that when we don't invite them, we are actually rejecting them from this part of our lives. We should be inviters, allowing others a chance to belong to the community of Jesus.

WHAT PART OF THE BODY ARE YOU?

God allowed the authors of the Bible to use their gifts of writing to create some unique word pictures. The apostle Paul, who wrote two thirds of the New Testament, used the Greek language to create beautiful word art that we still use to describe the church.

One especially well-known metaphor is the reference to the church being a body. It's described this way in 1 Corinthians 12:12-14:

> Just as a body, though one, has many parts, but all its many parts form one body, so it is with Christ. For we were all baptized by one Spirit so as to form one body—whether Jews or gentiles, slave or free—and we were all given the one Spirit to drink. Even so the body is not made up of one part but of many.

In verses 26 and 27 the passage continues. "If one part suffers, every part suffers with it; if one part is honored, every part rejoices with it. Now you are the body of Christ, and each one of you is a part of it." This metaphor is indispensable in helping us understand the important roles we play in the church. Every single person is a partner in and part of the body. The body doesn't work unless everyone participates in it; otherwise, it is broken. How many of our churches today are broken, even missing limbs, because only a few people are fully participating? Does this mean that everyone has to be a volunteer and serve in a particular way? No, but it means the church will thrive when every person within the community understands and is actively contributing to the mission of Jesus.

What opportunities exist for you to move from being an attender and consumer to being a contributor and builder? Serving opportunities within your student ministry are the launching point to finding your meaningful role in the body.

A few years ago, a teenager I worked with named Alex was in seventh grade. He had just started learning guitar and taking vocal lessons. That fall when we began to search for new members of the student worship team, Alex pursued the opportunity. Honestly, his first couple of months were tolerable, but far from great. Thankfully, with a strong affinity for music, the affirmation of the worship leader, and regular opportunity to practice, he kept at it. Several years later Alex was leading the whole student ministry worship team, as well as leading regularly on Sunday mornings.

In my house we have a measuring stick that we mark to determine how tall each one of our children has grown. Every six to twelve months we draw a new line to indicate our children's growth. Every time they grow, even if it's just a quarter inch, they are ecstatic. People want to know they are growing. One of the marks of spiritual growth is when someone moves from consumer to contributor. In the last few months have you measured your spiritual growth? I can guarantee that when you begin to play your meaningful role in the body, like Alex began to, not only will you grow, but as your spiritual muscles are stretched your heart will fill with joy.

THE DIFFERENCE BETWEEN ROLES AND GIFTS

Have you ever attended a church service and asked the question, "Why do we do things this way?" At some point in church history the early followers of Jesus began to structure the worship experience. At first, they just met, prayed, listened to teaching, and then ate together, as seen in Acts 2. Somewhere around the fourth century the people designed worship services. A worship service is simply a series of programmed elements that helped people encounter and worship Jesus, experiencing fellowship with him and with each other. For the past 1,600 years we have been putting up church buildings and creating worship structures that we think will serve the ministry of the church.

The modern Sunday morning service typically has several elements, among them singing, prayer, taking an offering, possibly a video, a sermon, more prayer, and then departure, all wrapped up into a neat hour or hour and a half experience.

On any given Sunday in North America you will generally see greeters who welcome people, ushers who pass the offering plate, worship team members who play instruments, a pastor who preaches, a technology team of people who run presentations and sound, adults who watch children and teach Sunday school, and a hospitality team that serves coffee and snacks. All of these roles exist to allow the structure of the church to function.

Many of these roles can be filled by anyone, regardless of what gifts they possess. There is no spiritual gift of technology required to push the button to advance a worship slide, for instance. However, while the roles don't *require* spiritual gifts, they do create opportunities for you to *use* your spiritual gifts. Do you know what spiritual gift is required to be an usher? Absolutely none. However, if you have the spiritual gift of hospitality, which means to welcome the stranger, then you may see welcoming a new person as one way of actively using that gift. In that brief interaction, that person may encounter the Holy Spirit working through you. You have effectively helped create heart space for someone to encounter Jesus through the preaching ministry of the pastor (who hopefully has the spiritual gift of teaching).

Many people find little to no joy in serving in a volunteer role. A primary reason leaders have a hard time recruiting volunteers to fill the roles that allow the structure of church to work is that people don't feel a spiritual affinity for the roles. They don't see how their service is going to make significant spiritual change. But when people know their spiritual gifts, and their importance in the body of Christ, they see volunteer roles as opportunities to participate in the mission of Jesus.

I'd encourage you as a young leader to embrace a greater understanding of how you can help fill the needs in the church, like Alex did in the section above. One thing you can do is to make a list of all the existing volunteer roles in the church or youth group. (I strongly recommend you take a whole church approach, even though I'm sure there are needs within your youth group as well.) Examine each opportunity and ask yourself, *What spiritual gifts would be most needed in this role? If that spiritual gift was present in that role how would that bring about spiritual change in the lives the people who attended the church?*

You can also think about how to create new meaningful roles centered around the gifts you possess. This may mean adjusting the structure of a service, helping create new teams and ministries in your youth group, or inviting others with the right gifts to fill the existing roles. There is certainly a need for roles anyone can fulfill, because they act as baby pools for people who are learning how to swim. But as anyone with children can tell you, every kid wants to get in the deep end, even if they express hesitation. Each of us knows there is more joy in jumping off a diving board than standing ankle deep in the water.

BEING DEPENDABLE

Can you recall the last time someone let you down? My guess is that it wasn't all that long ago. Parents, coaches, teachers, friends, and pastors will all, at one point or another, let us down. Can you recall the last time you let someone down? There is a significant amount of personal disappointment when we fail to honor our commitments. Often, we feel worse when we disappoint others than we do when others have let us down.

Not long ago I was traveling for work to Orlando, Florida, and I promised my children I would bring them something from my trip. I thought for sure they would want some kind of Disney toy, but before I could say another word my oldest daughter made a clear suggestion (okay, it was really more of a demand) that I bring home Sour Flush Pops.

These are plunger-shaped lollipops you dip into a sour powder dumped inside a mini plastic toilet bowl. Without being too crass, they taste like crap. Nonetheless, kids are kids and they like strange candies. Before I knew it, all five of my kids wanted Sour Flush Pops, and I was on the hook to deliver. I have seen these candies all over the place. When I landed in Orlando I went to a gas station to buy some, to no avail. They were out.

Five gas stations and several stores later I still had no Sour Flush Pops. At the end of my trip, I boarded the return flight, assuming I would be able to find them at the gas station near our house where I had seen them before. Again my plan was thwarted: they were sold out. Not wanting to disappoint my kids, I purchased a few similar candies instead.

Somewhat defeated, I went home. As I walked in the door all five kids ran up and gave me hugs, then immediately demanded their Sour Flush Pops. Sheepishly, I told them I couldn't find any and was sorry. Then I pulled out the replacement candies I was sure would assuage the bad news. Instead, a massive meltdown ensued.

Later that night I was putting the daughter who made the suggestion to bed. She was throwing some serious shade. When I asked her what was wrong she said, "Dad, I'm just disappointed. I was really depending on you to bring home my candy." I felt crushed. Then I told her, "Honey, if this is the only time I let you down, we will be in good shape." I knew in my heart that there would be bigger disappointments ahead. While we can't be one hundred percent reliable, and will all have our own Sour Flush failures, we should do our best to be dependable. I have since been on many other trips and have delivered the goods my kids requested. I try to follow through on what I say I'm going to do, and not make promises I can't keep.

Jesus urges his followers to be direct with our language. In Matthew 5:37 he says, "All you need to say is simply 'Yes' or 'No'; anything beyond this comes from the evil one." Vague expectations leave room for misunderstanding. When you are asked something and respond with "maybe," "it's possible," or "I'll try" instead of being up front about what you are thinking, you are creating space in your relationships for discord. It's a mistake to commit when you know you don't want to, or you can't fulfill a commitment wholeheartedly. This creates situations in which people are dependent on your full participation, but will only be given half or less.

What I love about this statement is that Jesus is giving you permission to say no to things you aren't one hundred percent able to commit to.

Being a part of the body of believers is not about committing to every single event, program, or ministry. It's about committing to fulfilling the mission of Jesus according to your gifts.

When you invite people into your ministry or ask them to serve, always respect their option to decline. Both you and they will be better off for it. And when you are asked to serve, don't be afraid to say no. Be a dependable person, someone whose yes and no are reliable. And allow grace to reign when circumstances outside of your control leave you or someone else disappointed.

EAT TOGETHER OFTEN

As you read the New Testament you will see that Jesus loved food. He ate both before his death and after his resurrection. Jesus, on separate occasions, fed 5,000 and 4,000 people. He turned water into wine as his first miracle, and he had a last supper. The greatest tell of all is that he gave us the sacrament of Communion, which involves eating bread and drinking wine together in remembrance of Jesus and his sacrifice.

In our modern context Jesus is often depicted as a relatively thin person, but in my imagination he has a little bit of a belly. He loved food too much to be shredded. As I read the Bible, I've wondered: why was Jesus always eating? Yes, eating is a communal and cultural activity, and yes, he walked a lot, which made him hungry. But did you know that Jesus got hangry? *Hangry* is slang for the feeling you get when you are hungry to the point of significant irritability. As Snickers advertised in a hilarious series of commercials, "You aren't you when you're hungry."

Enjoy this well documented account of Jesus's hanger found in Mark 11:12-14:

> The next day as they were leaving Bethany Jesus was hungry. Seeing in the distance a fig tree in leaf, he went to find out if it had any fruit. When he reached it, he found nothing but leaves, because it was not the season for figs. Then he said to the tree, "May no one ever eat fruit from you again."

Jesus, in his frustration, cursed the tree. That's a bad day to be a fig tree! The passage continues in verse 15. "Upon reaching Jerusalem, Jesus entered the temple courts and began driving out those who were buying and selling there. He overturned the tables of the money changers and the benches of those selling doves."

I don't share this passage about the fig tree to make light of Jesus. I share it to display the reality of human nature. He was hungry and he was angry. He used his hunger and anger in the most righteous way he could, by defending the temple and holding people accountable to the temple rules. His hanger became a holy anger. While there are deeper meanings to the story of the fig tree in Jesus's life, and regardless of whether you're with me on Jesus's hanger, one thing is certain: food was and is important.

Eating together is meaningful. It's something the earliest disciples did regularly. Acts 2:46 says, "Every day they continued to meet together in the temple courts. They broke bread in their homes and ate together with glad and sincere hearts." When we sit down and eat together it slows our pace and creates space for community. Even if the food tastes terrible, we are still part of a shared experience. Eating together is a way in which we show dignity and friendship to one another.

In Luke 14, Jesus shares a parable about a king who prepares a dinner banquet. When he invites his friends, they all decline his offer. They are too busy and don't want to be bothered. Angry, the king sends his servants out into the town to bring in anyone who may want to eat. Before you know it the banquet hall is filled with all sorts of people. He orders his servant to invite people from the streets and the alleys, "the poor, the crippled, the blind, and the lame" (Luke 14:21). The servant is instructed to continue inviting people until the table is full.

Who we invite to our tables says quite a bit about us. When we share a meal with someone, we are giving that person the gift of importance: that person is worth our time. This parable above has many meanings, but one thing we can draw from it is that our tables are not meant to be exclusive. Who are we eating with, and how often are we eating with them? Are we showing willingness to be hospitable?

Reflection Questions: Own Your Role in Church

1. This chapter emphasizes being an inviter. What kinds of things do we do as a youth group that provide good opportunities for us to invite others?

2. When was the last time you invited someone to something we did as a youth group? If this is hard for you, explain.

3. Make sure everyone has a piece of paper and something to write on. Each person should write the first and last names of their "Five Most Wanted"—that is, five friends you'd like to see come to youth group and come to have faith in Jesus.

4. As a group, take time going around the circle with each person praying for the "most wanted" people by name.

5. One idea another youth group uses to help new people feel welcome is this: all student leaders are required to, at least once during the evening or event, leave their normal circle of friends and interact with someone new or someone they don't normally speak with. At their upcoming student leader meeting, they are accountable to name the person or people they spoke with. Is this something we should try?

SECTION III:
CREATING

Using Your Gifts To Transform Community

Student leaders are growing as ones who trigger flourishing in others.

In the creation narrative in Genesis chapters 1 and 2 we see the power, beauty, and wonder of God. With his words he speaks into existence the heavens and the earth, the greatest creative experience in history. The most masterful piece of his creation is human beings. And one gift he gives to all of us is an invitation to be active cocreators in the world.

Leaders create spaces, experiences, language, and actions that move people and shape culture. As an active participant in the body of Christ, you will discover opportunities to create that will help people see and experience God. This section explores creating in ways that allow us to flourish as student leaders, and to find deep and meaningful expressions of our faith.

7 Culture Creation

STUDENT LEADERSHIP MATTERS

God loves student leaders. All throughout the Bible God calls young men and women to take faith-filled risks that transform whole communities and bring him glory and honor. It's easy to think of everyone in the Bible as a middle-aged adult, but God constantly uses young leaders to do things no one expects.

Jeremiah was only seventeen years old when God called him to be a prophet. These words from the first chapter of Jeremiah are powerful: "Before I formed you in the womb I knew you, and before you were born I set you apart; I appointed you as a prophet to the nations" (Jeremiah 1:5). Can you imagine being told by God that before you were even a thought in your parents' minds he already had a plan to use you to change the world? Jeremiah is certainly taken aback by it. "Alas, Sovereign LORD," he says in the next verse. "I can't speak for you! I'm too young!" Our natural tendency is to try and get out of our calling because we aren't sure we have what it takes.

Jeremiah argued with God's plan based on his age (though in the end he was faithful to what God was calling him to). Often, student leaders do the same. What list of disqualifications comes to mind when you think about serving God with your whole life? How many "what if" scenarios play out in your head? It's common for leaders to fight their calling because of their personal fears and because they often aren't certain of their own value.

Let's look at the book of Samuel in the Old Testament. Samuel was just a boy when the Lord spoke to him for the first time. He was about twelve years old and serving as an assistant to the high priest Eli when he heard the voice of God saying "Samuel! Samuel!" (1 Samuel 3:10). Thankfully Samuel was listening because he responded with, "Speak, for your servant hears." Samuel went on from that day forward listening for the voice of the Lord and creating fantastic societal transformation in the nation of Israel.

Mary was the mother of Jesus. When God spoke to her for the first time she was between thirteen and fifteen years old. As a teenage woman she was chosen for the highest possible honor when God asked her to bear into the world the Messiah. We aren't given much detail about how she raised Jesus, but we can see in his life the honor and respect he showed to women in a culture where women were considered second-class citizens. Jesus had close female friends, spoke to women who were considered outcasts, and encouraged women to be leaders in their communities. We can assume his love of and respect for women were nurtured and influenced, at least in part, by his mother.

All three of these young leaders—Jeremiah, Samuel, and Mary—were chosen by God. Each of them played major parts in shaping the cultures in which they lived.

You may not think of yourself as a Jeremiah, Samuel, or Mary, but don't discount what the Lord may have in store for you. The apostle Paul admonished Timothy, another young leader, for thinking the same way: "Don't let anyone look down on you because you are young, but set an example for the believers in speech, in conduct, in love, in faith and in purity" (1 Timothy 4:12). You are being invited as a young leader today to be an active example—before your family, friends, church, and youth group—of what can happen when a teenager becomes a sold-out follower of Jesus.

CULTURE IS MORE POWERFUL THAN PROGRAMS

Key influencing factors in your decision making, and who you are becoming, are the cultures you live in and identify with. The local church you attend has its own distinct culture; your school has its own culture; your group of friends has its own culture. You may live in the South and be part of Southern culture. Each of the cultures we are part of has simultaneous impact upon us. You are constantly navigating a world of co-cultures, each one with distinct patterns of influence in your life.

Leaders are creators and champions of the best things in their culture. An old teaching statement says, "More is caught than taught." This statement alludes to the power of cultural transformation. We learn more from what we observe and experience than from what's explicitly explained to us.

A few years ago I taught a series on prayer to our middle schoolers. The focus was on how, why, and when to pray, and on helping them understand how prayer influences the spiritual world within and around them. I spent four weeks teaching on this, and at the end of those four weeks my desired outcome was that they would be a group of youth who prayed. At the end of four weeks, four messages, and four small group times, no one was praying, at least not the way I wanted.

Thankfully, there was Matthew K., a seventh grader, who suggested we as a group pray at the end of our gatherings for five to ten minutes. It took several months of regularly doing this before we started to see a large number of middle schoolers staying ten or fifteen minutes later per night to pray for their friends, families, schools, and the world. It took time to create a culture in which prayer was a primary value and practice. If it wasn't for Matthew K., that cultural shift wouldn't have happened. The youth saw prayer as a normal behavior for middle schoolers once they saw peers of theirs who wanted to pray.

When specific behaviors, values, and positive or negative characteristics are normal in the groups we belong to, we are likely to adopt them as our own. If we wish to create cultures that make the group more like Jesus then we have to get the majority of the group to adopt the behaviors, values, and characteristics of Jesus. Is there an opportunity for you and some others to begin shaping culture by adopting and modeling the behaviors of Jesus within your group?

CREATE EXPECTATIONS WITHIN THE COMMUNITY

Every group you belong to has written or unwritten expectations. Expectations are the guidelines that inform people in the community what role they fill. Good leaders define clear expectations in every group in which they belong. When the expectations are clear, then each member is aware of and accountable to fulfill their role in order to meet the needs of the group. When good and clear expectations are set out and each member lives into them, there will be incredible transformation within each person and the larger community.

A few years ago I was reflecting on all that God had accomplished among the teenagers I had been serving. We had seen seventy-four youth say yes to Jesus as their friend for the first time over the previous twelve months. This was an amazing work of God. As a coworker and I discussed this incredible life transformation I was seeing, he made a comment. "Dan, with the number of students you work with, did you expect God to do less?" This subtle, friendly rebuke was exactly what I needed to hear. Often, our expectations of God are far less than what he tells us we can expect from him. God doesn't work in the world of unspoken expectations, he operates in the world of explicit and written expectation. He uses the Bible to lay out exactly what you can expect from him, and in return what he expects of you.

When you see God making a promise to people in the Bible, he is saying, "This is what you can expect from me." When we make God's promises the foundation of the expectations in our community, the power of God is prevalent and life transformation will begin to occur. In the pages to follow are several expectations that define the mission of Jesus. These expectations should be hallmarks of every group in which we belong.

Expectation #1: Come as You Are

When grace and understanding abound, the church becomes the primary community in which everyone can belong. Jesus does not ask anyone to change before being accepted. He accepts people regardless of their history, experiences, or behaviors. Jesus's promise for this expectation is found in Matthew 11:28-29, where he says, "Come to me, all you who are weary and burdened, and I will give you rest. Take my yoke upon you and learn from me, for I am gentle and humble in heart, and you will find rest for your souls." There are no prerequisites; we are simply invited to come to Jesus.

Expectation #2: Be Transformed

The church is a community in which you can come as you are, and then experience freedom from sin and whole-life transformation. Romans 6:14 says, "For sin shall no longer be your master, because you are not under the law, but under grace." When grace enters into someone's life through friendship with Jesus, a new work of transformation is underway. The promise of God is that he will continue to be at work in us throughout our lives. "...he who began a good work in you will carry it on to completion until the day of Christ Jesus" (Philippians 1:6).

Expectation #3: Make a Difference

The key to belonging rests in playing your meaningful role in the community. Each person is asked to step into a role in accordance with his or her gifts. When we create space for using our gifts, whole-life transformation accelerates and the mission of Jesus moves forward. Jesus promises us this: "Very truly I tell you, whoever believes in me will do the works I have been doing, and they will do even greater things than these..." (John 14:12).

EMBRACE THE UPSIDE DOWN OF CHRISTIANITY

Pretty much everything Jesus instructs us to do may feel counterintuitive. This is because of our spiritually defective DNA. It may feel like Christianity is upside down, because Jesus often takes the standard operating procedures of the world and flips them on their heads. This can feel uncomfortable, confusing, and even conflicting. But when we live according to the upside down, it makes the world right side up.

We can see clear examples of this in the Sermon on the Mount, which lays out the expectations for what the kingdom of God looks like. Jesus begins his sermon with what are commonly known as the Beatitudes (Matthew 5:3-11).

The word *Beatitude* means "supreme blessing." Each phrase Jesus shares starts with "Blessed are those…" In other words, "those who live like this will be blessed beyond measure in their lives on this earth." However, these Beatitudes don't make sense. They call us to lives of selflessness, which is difficult in a world where we predominately focus on ourselves.

The easiest way to understand the Beatitudes is to read them and then rewrite them from a humanistic point of view. In doing this, it's easy to see that the upside down of Christianity creates communities of belonging and transformation, while the kingdom of humans is elitist, exclusive, and harmful to ourselves and others.

Jesus: Blessed are the poor in spirit, for theirs is the kingdom of heaven.
Human Nature: You must be rich in talent, ability, wealth, and fame to inherit the kingdom of this world.

Jesus: Blessed are those who mourn, for they will be comforted.
Human Nature: Become hard, uncaring, and detached. Don't show weakness, for then you will be considered strong.

Jesus: Blessed are the meek, for they will inherit the earth.
Human Nature: Never be submissive to a higher authority, because you are the authority. Follow your heart at all costs and you will have all of its desires met.

Jesus: Blessed are those who hunger and thirst for righteousness, for they will be filled.
Human Nature: Hunger after selfishness and thirst for power and you will find temporary satisfaction, though you will never have

enough.

Jesus: Blessed are the merciful, for they will be shown mercy.
Human Nature: Hold grudges, seek revenge, and win at any cost, because the world gives glory to winners and treats losers harshly.

Jesus: Blessed are the pure in heart, for they will see God.
Human Nature: When you place yourself above others then you will realize you are your own God.

As we saw in chapter 4, the greatest commandment in Scripture is found in Matthew 22:37-39:

> 'Love the Lord your God with all your heart and with all your soul and with all your mind.' This is the first and greatest commandment. And the second is like it: 'Love your neighbor as yourself.' All the Law and the Prophets hang on these two commandments.

These words instruct us to make God and then others the recipients of our greatest love and devotion. The tendency of humanity, though, is to say, "Love yourself with all of yourself, and treat others in a way that benefits you."

As a growing leader, the temptation will be there to get the world to serve you, instead of serving the world. Like moths to a light, we are constantly drawn to being inwardly-focused people. We must constantly push outward. To do that we must keep our eyes first on Jesus, and model his heart for the world. As we do we shape the cultures around us into expressive environments of the kingdom of God.

BE IMMERSED IN THE WHOLE CHURCH

There is a popular GIF of a foot by the side of a pool. The big toe grows fifteen inches to dip down into the water to test it out. I use it a lot in my group chats because it signifies the position so many people take when they are invited to participate in activities where they aren't sure they belong. They are unwilling to jump in. They want assurance that the water is warm. Many teenagers do the same thing when they are invited to be a part of the "big church."

I call it "big church" hesitantly. The church has increasingly tended to do ministry differently for different generations. There is children's ministry, student ministry, men's and women's ministry, worship ministry, and the list goes on. The bigger the church, the greater the segregation of environments, by age and by other categories. These segregated ministry experiences that cater to special interest groups can be useful for discipleship, but they also scream, "You don't belong here!" to everyone who doesn't match the criteria.

When you think about your church, are there any environments you would be hesitant to jump into? Sometimes, it's not that you wouldn't be welcome, but that people wouldn't know what to do if you started showing up. The downside of this kind of structure is that when churches have specific ministries for people who fit specific demographics, they can lose a whole-church perspective. Many studies on millennials and Generation Z indicate that these generations are leaving the church.[7,8] After youth group and high school graduation, they will not find a church. This exodus is not necessarily what anyone wants, but it is the consequence of people of this generation not knowing where they belong outside of their specific group.

When I was eighteen years old I moved from Philadelphia to Chicago to pursue my undergraduate studies at Moody Bible Institute. In Philadelphia my church experience was spent in children's and then youth ministry. Rarely did I ever engage in the church outside of those groups. If adults hadn't entered those spaces to be with me, then my interactions with adults would have been nonexistent.

Then, as a young adult in Chicago, I was expected to become part of the larger church. This was an appealing and scary venture. As I started attending and looking for a new "church home" I realized one thing: I didn't belong. Because of my age and inability to relate well with adults outside of my contextualized environments, I was seen as too young for adult ministry, but too old for youth ministry.

Additionally, I couldn't find a church with a young adult ministry. I had to make a choice. I would either stay home and not go to church, or make myself fit somewhere. I wanted to be on mission with Jesus, and I wanted to do it with other people, so I chose to try to fit in, no matter how emotionally uncomfortable that was going to be.

I quickly learned the value of helping people belong. Belonging isn't easy. It takes a genuine commitment to find a place in a church where you didn't grow up. Belonging doesn't happen quickly. It's is the byproduct of time, the development of relationships, and the discovery of a role to play in the community. With enough time and consistent engagement, I was able to make friends, and eventually find a role in the community to fill. Finally, after about a year, I belonged.

Not many people would work that hard to belong to a church community. I did it because church attendance was mandatory for me as a student at MBI. But most people don't have to meet that expectation. As a student leader one of the greatest gifts you can give your church is being involved in areas beyond student ministry. If the church is a body, then every part needs to participate for the overall health of the body. You are making your church healthier simply by being present and engaging in more of it. And, if you ever leave the church you are currently attending, it will give you insight and perspective on how to find belonging and help others do the same in other church contexts.

If you are active in the student ministry, are you also active in the women's ministry or men's ministry? Do you volunteer with the tech team, help with children's ministry, or play with the Sunday morning worship team? It's difficult to push into the parts of the church that don't seem to be designed for you, but the Bible teaches that the whole church is for you. As a young leader the time to immerse yourself in the whole church is now. If you wait until you leave high school to become part of the whole body, you will have a difficult transition ahead.

When you enter other parts of the church, you are helping other teenagers know they belong in those spaces too. Leadership is about allowing your talents and gifts to be used in every part of the body. When you engage in the whole church you are shifting the status quo of church expectation and creating a culture of belonging.

Reflection Questions: Culture Creation

1. As a group, list the categories of gatherings you typically have. For example, a group might list *Sunday School, weekly youth group, monthly extra event, weekend retreat, annual mission trip,* etc. What do you believe is the "feel" or "culture" of each of these different kinds of gatherings?

2. What is your contribution to a positive feeling in each of these settings? For example, in a weekly youth group meeting one contribution might be to enthusiastically support whatever is going on up front (worship, a game, teaching, etc.).

3. Of the three expectations listed in the chapter explain which is your favorite and why.
   • Come as you are
   • Be transformed
   • Make a difference

4. Are we weak in any of the three areas? If so, how can we improve in the coming month?

8 Leading Others

MAKE THE SHIFT FROM RECEIVER TO GIVER

You probably know the saying "It is more blessed to give than to receive." This is actually Jesus speaking a Beatitude as quoted by Paul in Acts 20:35. There is no question that we live in a consumer culture. Humans are consumers by nature. We have been since the creation. We consume the fruits and animals of the land, acquire goods, and stockpile things away if we can. We do the same thing in our interpersonal relationships.

Relational consumerism is why reality TV is so popular. We consume other people's drama, excitement, fear, and joy in short segments. In our personal lives, we have friends from whom we consume something. We consume their time, and benefit emotionally from them. We may also consume their physical goods. Have you ever had that one friend whose house seemed to have everything? A pool and hot tub, the always-filled cookie jar, that monster theater room, the latest video game system, a four-wheeler or go-kart... You like him for more than his house, but the house, and everything in it, is a great side benefit of the friendship.

When relationships center on what we can get from people instead of how we can invest in people, they become expendable. As soon as we squeeze what we want from someone, we move on. We probably don't think of it in such blunt terms, but on some level, this is what is happening when we cycle through friendships or have serial dating relationships. Every relationship is providing something we are seeking. It could be a sense of security, self-worth, physical pleasure, or the meeting of any number of emotional or physical needs. When either person seeks to have her own needs met more than she focuses on the needs of the other person, the relationship quickly burns out.

As leaders in the church we will always be inviting other people to join us in accomplishing the mission of Jesus. It cannot be done alone, but it also cannot be done at the expense of other people. We have to diligently walk the line between partnering with others and using them. In my view, the single greatest passage in the Bible on this is in Ephesians 5:1-2. Traditionally this passage is used to teach on marriage, but it can also instruct us on the depth of relationship we can have with Jesus, the people in the church, and within our communities. Paul says, "Follow God's example, therefore, as dearly loved children, and walk in the way of love, just as Christ loved us and gave himself up for us as a fragrant offering and sacrifice to God." Jesus gave himself up for the sake of others. It cost him his time, energy, emotions, and eventually his very life. It is always costlier to devote ourselves to others for their sakes than it is to take from them for our own sakes, yet the example of Jesus is the one we are to follow.

A few years ago I started an internship program in our church. It was supposed to help us pursue extra ministry initiatives that couldn't be done without gifted people who could fulfill specific roles. Initially I wanted to bring on skilled people we could call interns, but actually treat like employees. Interns usually have limited skill sets, but potential for real success if they are developed. An employee, on the other hand, should already have the desired skills and need limited development. I personally wanted to see a big impact, but didn't want to do the difficult development work. This was a huge mistake. The first year of the program was mediocre at best because I didn't spend enough time helping the intern develop his skill sets. At the end of nine months he left feeling like he had wasted his time. He wanted me to invest in his life, but I had wanted to extract and gain. This led to the untimely end of the internship with both of us feeling frustrated.

Fortunately, the Lord worked in my heart regarding the internships. I needed to view these internships as discipleships. I had to invest in each young leader God had entrusted to me. The end result was that in four months my next intern was doing more than my previous intern had done in nine months. It had nothing to do with her initial capacity as a leader, and everything to do with me investing in her. The focus shifted from gaining to giving, and to growing her capacity and love for Jesus. Over four years I had four interns who all launched into full-time ministry at the end of their internships. Because I took the time to invest, they were able to bless our church for a season, but the kingdom of God for eternity.

Who has God placed in your life? Whose life can you invest in? Jesus had twelve disciples, and from those twelve there are now over two billion followers of Jesus around the world. When we take the time to invest in a few, we are creating eternal gain. Jesus was right: it is more blessed to give than to receive.

THE ART OF COLLABORATIVE LEADERSHIP

Have you ever worked on a group project? This is one of the least appealing homework assignments you can be given. Inevitably there will be certain group members frustrated and doing the majority of the work while the others simply reap the benefits. The one who takes on the most work usually has a strong desire to see a positive outcome. The others are relying on that person to deliver, but they don't have as much personal ownership in the outcome.

We need to understand that collaborative leadership is not about distributing the workload evenly, but creating equal ownership of the outcome of the project. When all members feel an equal amount of desire and the same degree of passion, they will take real ownership of the tasks they are assigned. Their contributions now have greater value to them personally.

BECOMING A STUDENT LEADER

There are very few things you'll get to do for Jesus that you'll be asked to do alone. Jesus's desire is that we would work together with the whole body of believers, using as many people as needed to accomplish the goals set before us. Collaborative leadership is about getting people to use their gifts and work together to achieve a goal that matters to all of them. When people share the same vision, it is much easier for them to see the value in the work they must do to see a project accomplished.

The early church knew quite a bit about collaborative leadership. Acts chapter 6 describes a problem pertaining to caring for the widows in the church in Jerusalem. Through collaborative leadership, the early church worked together to create a shared vision and a successful outcome. The workloads were not even, but because the ownership was high for everyone the project was a huge success. Let's take a look at the key factors that allowed their collaborative leadership to succeed.

Identify the Opportunity or Problem To Be Solved
Once the group admits there is a problem, need, or opportunity they can begin to dream together about a solution.

The backstory comes from the book of Acts.

> In those days when the number of disciples was increasing, the Hellenistic Jews among them complained against the Hebraic Jews because their widows were being overlooked in the daily distribution of food. So the Twelve gathered all the disciples together and said, "It would not be right for us to neglect the ministry of the word of God in order to wait on tables." (Acts 6:1-2)

What was happening was this: the twelve disciples were entrusted with a specific ministry as apostles to preach and teach the word of God, advancing the mission of Jesus through evangelism. When certain Jews approached them asking for assistance in making sure the widows among them were taken care of, they identified an opportunity, but also a problem. They had an opportunity to build a system that could meet the needs of all the widows without favoring one group over another. But meeting these needs would pull the disciples away from their primary calling to preach the word and grow the church community. They would have to come up with another solution.

Create a Shared Vision

Unlike a group project that is assigned and must be completed, collaborative leadership starts with a problem that needs to be solved, and the group creates the project that will provide a solution.

The story continues:

> "…Brothers and sisters, choose seven men from among you who are known to be full of the Spirit and wisdom. We will turn this responsibility over to them and will give our attention to prayer and the ministry of the word." This proposal pleased the whole group. (Acts 6:3-5)

In this brief span of verses it's easy to miss the amount of time that probably went into this collaborative project proposal. The twelve disciples were together, and at some point they had to discuss the problem and dream up a solution. Most likely they had representatives from all of the groups involved in the conversation. Together they dreamed up a project that would allow the apostles to keep preaching and that would also address the community's growing needs: seven new leaders would be chosen to make sure the widows were cared for. Collaborative leadership should lead to projects and dreams that excite, use, and encourage the majority of people involved.

Assign Individual and Corporate Ownership of Projects and Tasks

Each person has different gifts. When the tasks meet the giftings available, then work is a joy. Everyone knows what he or she is responsible for and that each role is important. If the project fails, there is no single person to blame.

The story continues:

> They chose Stephen, a man full of faith and of the Holy
> Spirit; also Philip, Procorus, Nicanor, Timon, Parmenas, and
> Nicolas from Antioch, a convert to Judaism. They presented
> these men to the apostles, who prayed and laid their hands
> on them. (Acts 6:5-6)

The men in this passage, who came from different segments of
the community representing the groups involved, were chosen to
collaboratively work on a project. Once these men were chosen
they were then given the authority to execute the project among the
widows by an authority higher than themselves, the apostles.

Measure and Celebrate the Outcomes

When a project is successful there will be tangible rewards and a deep
sense of accomplishment in the whole community.

The story concludes this way:

> So the word of God spread. The number of disciples in
> Jerusalem increased rapidly, and a large number of priests
> became obedient to the faith. (Acts 6:7)

In telling the outcome of this story, the text wasn't simply written to
say "all the widows were fed." There were other beautiful outcomes
too. As it says, the Word of God spread, the number of disciples
increased, and priests "became obedient" to the faith. This project
met people's tangible needs, but even more importantly it produced
eternal results. Bringing others into relationship with Jesus is the
primary focus of all collaborative projects within the church. When
the world sees how well we love one another, whether with systems
of caring for widows or other humanitarian projects, it advances the
cause of the gospel. Physical projects should always have spiritual
outcomes.

When you reflect on the current projects your group is working on,
do they meet the criteria you set out for them? Where do you need to
go back and adjust current projects? What other opportunities exist
for your group to create projects that meet real needs, both tangible
and spiritual? Collaborative leadership can have a long learning

curve. However, the more you work together with others, the easier it will be to discern the direction you are to head in as a group, and the greater the spiritual outcomes you will experience.

STRETCHING: GROWING IN YOUR FLEXIBILITY

Being a flexible leader means being able to adjust a project, your personal perspective, or plans as necessary. We do not live in a static world. Things change every second of every day, and being adaptable is important.

A few years ago I was about to drive over a mountain pass in Colorado with my wife and five kids in the twelve-passenger van we affectionally call the #boalbus. We were returning from a relaxing weekend in Steamboat Springs, Colorado, a fun mountain getaway where you can soak in hot tubs and hot mineral water pools. We were refreshed and ready to go home. Little did we know, no amount of spa time was going to relax us enough to deal with the drive home. As we approached the pass, traffic stopped. The road was closed because of snow and ice. It was an immediate bummer.

Not wanting to be stuck in the mountains another night, my wife, Amy, quickly opened Google Maps to determine a new route. Once she charted the course we started again, heading toward a different pass. As we approached the second pass, the highway signs made us aware that the conditions there were even worse. Those roads were also closed. Several more hours of trying to circumnavigate the pass in bad weather and difficult traffic made for a very stressed out family. Everyone wanted out of the van.

We were only an hour from home but had no way of getting there. Frustrated and exhausted, we decided to find a hotel. The only problem was that all of the hotels were booked full of other travelers experiencing the same problem. We were tired, stuck, and miserable.

After pulling into the parking lot of a Subway, my wife and I made our last plan: we would pray that God would clear the original pass. A little while later as we reapproached the first pass, the state police were just starting to remove the road closed signs and open up travel

back through the pass. The Lord heard our prayer and answered—
or he just knew we would pray around the same time the weather
would clear up. Either way, it was a huge relief to know that we
would be home soon. When we got on the previously closed road the
conditions were still dangerous, but since so many people had chosen
not to cross the pass the traffic was minimal and it was a fairly easy
drive.

When we create a plan to fulfill a mission, it can be tempting to
execute the plan regardless of what the situation actually dictates.
Had my wife and I ignored the road closed signs, any number of
tragedies could have arisen. We weren't certain the road would open
back up or that another pass or road would get us home. But the
mission never changed: find a way home. We completed the mission,
though it took longer than expected, and we went around in circles
before we got there. The Lord made us wait for an open road, which
is what he often does. At just the right time he'll remove the obstacle
that's keeping a plan from being fulfilled.

Flexible leaders adjust their plans to ensure the success of the mission
at the least possible expense. Good leaders are willing to explore
other routes when the first one seems impassable. Finding a new
route or a hotel would have cost us more time and a few more dollars,
but it was worth infinitely less than our safety.

In hindsight, the other option was to wait, though we had no
indication that waiting for the pass to clear was a likely solution. I
think our roundabout journey was God's way of bringing us to the
point where we would recognize that we would only get home by
God's power. It was a lesson we needed to learn. We may be flexible
and have great plans, but it's still only by God's hand that those plans
prevail.

The flexible leader understands the greater costs involved in sticking
to the original plan regardless of how circumstances have changed.
It may be beneficial to sacrifice small things, make adjustments, and
try alternatives if they allow you to reach the main goal. The apostle
Paul was well aware of these types of scenarios. Often in his life,

things didn't go according to plan. He was shipwrecked, imprisoned, delayed, beaten, and stoned, all in his efforts to preach the gospel on his missionary journeys. Yet he was flexible enough to embrace the situations he faced and preach the gospel to whoever would listen, in whatever circumstances he found himself.

His flexibility is expressed in his exhortation to other leaders in Philippians 4:12-13:

> I know what it is to be in need, and I know what it is to have plenty. I have learned the secret of being content in any and every situation, whether well fed or hungry, whether living in plenty or in want. I can do all this through him who gives me strength.

In what situations have you found yourself inflexible? How has that impacted your most important goals? How you can you work with others to adjust? When you are a champion of flexibility it can make the detours just as rewarding.

EXPECT MORE OF YOURSELF BEFORE YOU EXPECT MORE FROM OTHERS

Whether it's at school, in your family, at youth group, on a sports team, or some other place, there will be times when you feel like you need other people to start pulling more weight.

There is a popular children's book called *The Giving Tree* by Shel Silverstein. A little boy befriends a tree, and over many years the tree gives the boy everything she has: her fruit, then her shade. As the boy grows he takes even more from the tree—her branches, her trunk— until the tree is just a stump. He leaves the tree alone for many years in between visits, returning only when he needs something. Finally, as a very old man he approaches the stump one last time. The tree says, "I have nothing left to give you," to which the old man replies, "I don't need very much now, just a quiet place to sit and rest." The final image is of the old man sitting on the stump. The book ends with the line, "and the tree was happy." The boy finally gave the tree the one thing she wanted all of those years: his companionship.[9]

Unfortunately, people are not giving trees. We cannot keep taking and expecting more without giving back an equal or greater amount. Leaders understand that when they ask a lot of others, they should also be giving a lot of themselves.

George Washington, the first president of the United States, was also a general. He never sent his men into battle without being present with them. He felt convicted that if his men were being asked to give it all, then no less should be expected of him. There are many historical accounts of George Washington riding his horse into battle ahead of his men. When he expected them to charge toward the enemy, he led the way. When he expected more from them, he also expected more of himself. In return his soldiers followed him loyally.

The book of Esther gives the account of a woman who never expected more from others than she did of herself. Esther was a Jewish slave concubine in the king's court. Her family was captured in the exile of Jerusalem by Nebuchadnezzar, the former king of Babylon. When Vashti, wife of the new king Xerxes, was driven out of the palace, the king began a search for a new queen. Esther knew she was in a unique position to potentially change the circumstances of her people. She was highly favored by Xerxes, and she became queen.

To enter the presence of the king and make requests without permission could have meant her death, but Esther placed her life on the line to bring about societal reform in Babylon. As queen, she requested that the execution sentence handed down for the complete annihilation of the Jewish people be stayed. The king listened, and issued a decree allowing all Jewish people to defend themselves without retribution if they were attacked by Babylonians. This new decree resulted in the salvation of the people.

Think of your current relationships. Are you currently asking others to do more than you are willing to do yourself? Leaders are constantly asking others to give greatly, pull more weight, or take on bigger roles. And the best leaders, like George Washington, like Esther, know that the more they give to their people, they more they will get from their people. Unless we are modeling a high degree of giving, we can't ask other people to give more.

DOUBLE HONOR

When you invite people to be part of a project or ministry, honor them appropriately. Honor is a biblical concept. It means to bestow upon someone a blessing for that person's work. It is an act of public or private recognition to help someone feel appreciated and respected.

Many people give verbal honors: words of praise, thankfulness, and encouragement. Most of the time that is more than appropriate. Occasionally, there will be times when you should give double honor, which means to match your verbal honor with a financial or physical gift.

A few years ago I was traveling and meeting with a few churches doing some consulting work. During my trip a church I had not planned on visiting contacted me and asked if I could swing by and offer some training. Since I was a few hours away and I happened to have the space in my schedule I agreed.

I walked through the seminars and then a Q & A and had a fine evening. As we wrapped up the session, a Domino's delivery car pulled up to the church. While I was packing up my things I received many verbal accolades from the attendees and the pastors. That's when the person who had invited me to come handed me a small pizza, something I could eat during my drive back to where I was staying. It was a double honor.

1 Timothy 5:17 says, "The elders who direct the affairs of the church well are worthy of double honor, especially those whose work is preaching and teaching." Paul is trying to encourage Timothy to bless those people financially for the extra work they are doing, as preaching and teaching take significant preparation and planning time.

Good leaders give honor to those they serve, but great leaders know when to give double honor. When I was a youth pastor, every other month I blessed my student leaders. I had a system built around four fundamental principles: develop, encourage, cast vision, and appreciate. Every two weeks my focus was on one of these areas. Notice that two of the four are founded on honoring the student leaders. This means at least once a month they were receiving verbal honors or a physical gift showing my appreciation. I gave out Starbucks cards, movie tickets, t-shirts, handwritten letters, and took them to lunch. These were committed youth who gave significant time to the ministry. Without them we couldn't have done half of what we did. They all received double honor, frequently. I use the same system today with the many people I serve with. It ensures they know I value everything they do.

Double honor does not have to be financial, it just has to be intentional. Who can you intentionally bless with a physical gift of appreciation for the service they are doing?

Reflection Questions: Leading Others

1. If you are on a sports team, in a music group, part of a drama production, or involved in any other "high commit-ment" activity, explain the requirements or expectations that come along with it. (For example, for a sports team one needs to come to practice.)

2. Along the same lines of the previous question, what do you think should be the agreed-upon commitments to be on this student leadership team? Think about this in terms of a few big categories of commitments: 1) to God, 2) to each other on the leadership team, 3) to the whole youth group, 4) to the adult leaders, and 5) to the whole church.

3. If you have witnessed the positive impact of high com-mitment involvement on a sports team, drama club, etc., explain what it feels like to be around high-commitment people.

4. Now translate that to youth group and being primarily a giver, not just a receiver. What impact will this have on you?

5. If you and the rest of the leadership team members be-came more committed to your youth group, what impact might that have on the rest of the group?

9 GOING FORWARD

LISTENING TO THE HOLY SPIRIT AND LEADING BY FAITH

Regularly, I can hear the Holy Spirit speaking to me. I have become accustomed to this voice and direction in my life, and it has increased the closeness I feel with Jesus. However, this wasn't always the case, and it isn't a day-to-day reality for most followers of Jesus. One of the things I spend time working on with teens is how to listen and respond to the voice of the Spirit, and I always start by reading the gospel of John with them. John's account of Jesus's life contains profound theology about listening for God's voice.

Most people desperately desire to hear the Lord speaking to them. The good news is that listening and hearing can, and should, be a normal part of following him. After all Jesus says in John 10:27, "My sheep listen to my voice; I know them, and they follow me."

But how does this happen? What does it look like? The Holy Spirit speaks to us in different ways, including through the written words of the Bible. Here are a few ways you can be listening to the voice of the Holy Spirit.

Focusing on the Word of God: Jesus

When you are reading the New Testament and see the word "Word," the Greek translation is *Logos*. *Logos* is regularly used in connection with a written or spoken proclamation of God. The disciple John was very fond of using the word *Logos* to refer to Jesus and his words. He starts John 1:1 by declaring, "In the beginning was the Word [Logos], and the Word [Logos] was with God, and the Word [Logos] was God." John's "Word of God" theology is an ongoing theme. John is emphasizing that Jesus himself utters the very words of God because he is God. Therefore, when we read or hear the words of Jesus and listen to them, we are listening to actual *Logos* (words) of God.

In John 12:49 Jesus says, "For I did not speak on my own, but the Father who sent me commanded me to say all that I have spoken." Since Jesus himself proclaims that his words are indeed from God the Father, it's no wonder why John refers to Jesus as the *Logos*. The Bible is referred to as the "Word of God," and Jesus is also referred to as the "Word of God."

You can begin listening by reading and understanding the teachings of Jesus. How do you see his teachings lived out in your own life? Do you see his values and commands present in the community in which you worship? Where do you see Jesus's values present throughout Scripture? When you look for and listen for Jesus's voice, you will recognize it all throughout the Bible.

Listening to the Holy Spirit in Prayer

One of my favorite quotes comes from Ernest Hemingway in *Across the River and into the Trees*. It says, "When people talk, listen completely. Don't be thinking about what you're going to say. Most people never listen."[10] How often have you felt lost and confused when following Jesus? How often have you felt like he was distant and silent? These feelings arise when we don't take time to listen to the Holy Spirit.

Make space in your life to simply listen. Go into prayer with no plan other than to listen for what God might be trying to tell you. In 1 Kings 19 we see that God speaks to Elijah in a whisper. Elijah had to be still, quiet enough to hear the soft whisper of the Holy Spirit. When is the last time you were quiet enough to hear the Holy Spirit speaking to your heart? Take time daily to be quiet and listen.

Paying Attention To Your Dreams

Most nights we can't remember our dreams. Sometimes our dreams scare us witless, and other times our dreams feel so real it seems impossible they aren't true. In the Bible we see examples of people like Joseph and Paul having visions and dreams, and God still speaks through dreams and visions today.

In 2012 I had a dream that I would give a million dollars to international mission work. In this dream I was sitting at a desk writing a check, then handing it to people in other nations. By 2016 I had done just that. It's not because I won the lottery, or had a handsome payday. A few months after the dream I was given the role of missions pastor, overseeing a budget that gave about $300,000 a year to overseas mission work. God used that dream to place in me a desire to give a million dollars to international mission work, and prepare my heart to be entrusted with the oversight of that much money.

What dreams has God given you? Have you seen them prepare your heart for future things God may have in store? Try keeping a dream journal and see what happens.

Wise Counsel in the Form of Recollection

The Holy Spirit might bring to mind Scripture you have memorized. These recollections come at times when you need encouragement or help overcoming temptation. It could even be one word or one phrase of Scripture that helps you make some decision. The Holy Spirit that indwells us often brings to mind the Scripture in our hearts to minister to us just as we need it.

Wise Counsel from Others

Throughout the book of Proverbs we are encouraged to seek the wise counsel of others. This is not asking other people to listen to the Holy Spirit for us, but to evaluate what you think the Lord is saying to you by running it by other people. Other friends of Jesus can help us assess quickly what we think we are hearing from Jesus and affirm it or help us rethink our perspective.

~~~~~~~~~~~~~~~~~~~~~~~~~~~

This is not an exhaustive list, but a platform to help you get started listening to the voice of the Holy Spirit. As a student leader and a person who is friends with Jesus, listening for the voice of God should be part of your everyday life. Christian leaders have the opportunity to be active listeners, not just to people but to the Holy Spirit. What would it look like for you to create listening space?

One of my least favorite phrases is "reading the Bible." It's time for all of us to stop asking only how often we are reading the Bible and start asking how often we are taking time to listen to Jesus. When you are in the habit of listening to Jesus you will naturally know how to follow him, and help others do the same.

TAKING RISKS—AS A TEAM

Many years ago I had a desire to host a See You at the Pole rally (a start-of-the-school-year gathering of Christian teenagers) at our church. There was nothing like that in our region, and I felt prompted by the Holy Spirit to make this our next big initiative. Our student ministry team had never been to one or hosted one, but I felt like we had the opportunity to bring multiple churches in our community together for a night of worship, prayer, and celebration to kick off the new school year. God was asking me to take a risk and try something new to advance his mission.

When God asks us to do something, he is never asking us to do it alone. It takes all parts of the body to complete what he sets out for us. Unfortunately, I didn't act like I believed this. I thought for sure I could pull off this event with minimal help.

I was planning a large rally, anticipating hundreds of teenagers from our community attending. There would be an amazing concert, fun stage and crowd games, door prizes, and powerful testimonies and prayer. Events like this take a lot of people, many different gifts, and significant buy-in from others. In my ignorance, I thought I could invite people to attend, but not invite them to participate in making it happen.

As the time drew close for the event, my co-pastor, Clayton, and I spent weeks going from church to church, inviting other youth pastors in the area to join in. We held a meeting of area-wide leaders, and poorly cast a vision for what God could do at this event. I actually stopped Clayton midway through his invitation and took over because I thought he wasn't doing a good enough job motivating others to participate. We looked unorganized and untrustworthy. We told everyone we would handle everything and all they had to do was put it on their schedule and attend, then let God do the rest. Several youth pastors offered to help in some way. I think they saw what we couldn't: we were in trouble. I declined, believing I was doing them a service by not burdening their workload.

We had planned to have 400-500 people present, and were expectant that God was going to do something amazing. To my embarrassment and frustration we ended up with about sixty people. My own youth group barely showed up! No one knew the songs the band played, because they played songs from their album and not worship songs. Clayton and I were visibly frustrated with each other because I went off script and neglected the order of service we had planned. A teenager did pray, which was good, but the energy had completely left the room. We were trying too hard and everyone knew it. The entire night was a total disaster, and I felt like God really let me down. After all, I took a faith-filled risk and expected a faith-filled outcome.

The next morning, I didn't even want to get out of bed. My pride was hurt. I had failed at what I thought God wanted me to do. As I was driving into church, processing my disappointment by praying and yelling at God, I heard him tell me, "Try again, but not alone." A few minutes later I arrived at the church. I was scared to debrief the event with Clayton. I knew what was coming. He was going to give me an earful about all the things I hadn't done right, and I deserved every bit of it. Thankfully, instead he showed me a lot of grace. He asked, "Do you want to try again? If we do, what are we going to do differently?" My immediate response was that yes I did—and that next time we wouldn't do it alone.

Holding the See You at the Pole rally the following year was an even bigger risk. Those who came the year before knew how bad of an event it was, and those whose help I'd turned down before felt unappreciated and undervalued. There was a good chance they would ignore the new invite all together. However, I was encouraged by 1 Corinthians 12:14: "...the body is not made up of one part but of many." With a lot of prayer, and a lot of apologies, we set forth on the adventure of planning the next event together. With the input of four other youth pastors we created a whole community prayer campaign and outreach night. This time, I felt no anxiety and had greater confidence that I was doing what the Lord had asked me to. The rally was a success, and for the next several years we saw over a thousand teenagers gather at this annual event to pray, worship, and be on mission together in our community.

Taking faith-filled risks is one of the most exciting things about being a follower of Jesus. It's a risk because failure is a real possibility. But failure is almost guaranteed when we think our gifts, talents, passions, and skills alone are enough. As the saying goes, "If you want to go fast go alone, but if you want to go far go together."

I like to reflect on the words Jesus spoke to his disciples before sending them out on a risk-filled mission in Matthew 10:16: "I am sending you out like sheep among wolves." Jesus did not send his disciples on a risky mission alone—he sent the twelve disciples together. When you examine the dreams God has placed on your heart for your ministry or community, who else is being invited into the mission? I can guarantee Jesus isn't asking you to go alone.

LEADERS ARE LEARNERS

Leadership development is a lifelong process. You will never know all that you need to know to do everything God is asking you to do. Focusing on learning from the past, learning from personal failure, and learning from those who are older will help you continue growing as a leader and follower of Christ.

Learning from the Past

There is an old saying: "Those who do not learn history are doomed to repeat it." Since hindsight is always 20/20, we can look to the past for guidance in making decisions now. Deuteronomy 32:7 encourages knowledge of and reflection on the past:

Remember the days of old;
  consider the generations long past.
Ask your father and he will tell you,
  your elders, and they will explain to you.

God gave this commandment to the Israelites so that they would remember all that he had done to rescue them from captivity and oppression. By learning the history of their people, they could apply their knowledge and avoid the same outcomes in the future.

As leaders in your community it would be wise to learn from your national, regional, church, and family histories. Ask questions. What significant events occurred in your community that influenced the culture? What was your church like when it first started? Who in your family lineage took big risks, and how did they turn out? Why were the laws of your town or city created, and how well do they work? Seeking answers to these types of questions can help develop a greater perspective from which you can make sound decisions.

Learning from Personal Failure

No one likes to learn the hard way. But from our failures we can gain great wisdom. Proverbs 26:11 says, "As a dog returns to its vomit, so fools repeat their folly." When we don't learn from past mistakes, we are acting foolishly.

When we take the time to evaluate failure, we find value in the brokenness. One of the gifts of friendship with Jesus is the gift of redemption. Jesus is constantly redeeming the broken things in this world for his glory and our benefit. When we let people down, hurt others with our words, or participate in things that lead to feelings of guilt and shame, we can then allow Jesus into the mix. If we seek his wisdom and understanding, his grace will bring forth our transformation.

Have you taken the time to invite Jesus in as you evaluate your greatest failures? To speak to you on how things went wrong? When you do you will not find condemnation, but restoration.

Learning from Those Who Are Older

In the book of 1 Kings, Rehoboam becomes king of Israel. Rehoboam's father was Solomon. At the end of Solomon's rule the people were heavily taxed and burdened by the projects Solomon had initiated. Jeroboam, a representative of the people, approached Rehoboam and said, "Your father put a heavy yoke on us, but now lighten the harsh labor and the heavy yoke he put on us, and we will serve you" (1 Kings 12:4).

This was quite the request to hear within your first few months of becoming king. Jeroboam was throwing down an ultimatum: unless Rehoboam brought about tax reform, the nation would rebel against him. He was threatening civil war. Rehoboam decided to pursue the wise counsel of others. First, he spoke with his father's advisors, people of an older generation. They advised him to acquiesce. "If today you will be a servant to these people and serve them and give them a favorable answer, they will always be your servants" (1 Kings 12:7).

Rehoboam decided to get a second opinion. He asked his friends, peers around his own age. They responded differently: "Now tell them, 'My little finger is thicker than my father's waist. My father laid on you a heavy yoke; I will make it even heavier'" (1 Kings 12:10-11).

Who do you think Rehoboam listened to, and what do you think was the outcome? The elder advisors implored him to become a servant to the people and thereby win their allegiance. His friends suggested he increase the people's burden to receive more personal gain. In the end Rehoboam listened to his friends, and there was rebellion. The twelve tribes of Israel split into two nations, Israel (consisting of ten tribes that broke away) and Judah (consisting of two tribes that remained). Rehoboam's wealth would have been infinitely greater had the twelve tribes stuck together, but in disregarding the wisdom of the elders he lost nearly everything.

Who has God placed in your life as an elder? Your grandparents, parents, teachers, pastors, mentors, and coaches are all ahead of you in life, and have amassed life experiences from which you can draw. While our elders may sometimes offer poor counsel, it's still imperative that you seek out, listen to, and respect the advice of those who are older. Their years bring perspective you have not yet attained and can benefit from.

Learning from the past, learning from failure, and learning from an older generation can all contribute to wise decisions. This learning doesn't guarantee success, but operating without it guarantees failure. Good leaders are always looking for ways to learn and grow.

SOMETHING MORE PRECIOUS THAN GOLD (WISDOM)

Wisdom is so precious to God's heart that he dedicated five books of the Bible to it: Ecclesiastes, Job, Song of Songs, Psalms, and Proverbs. With this much of the Bible dedicated to it, it makes sense that we as followers of Jesus should become lovers of wisdom. By wisdom I mean the ability to know the difference between what is right and wrong and then choose to do what is right.

The life of King Solomon illustrates the value and the difficulty of attaining wisdom and living wisely. As a young man and the new king of Israel, the Lord appeared to Solomon in a dream and offered him anything he wanted. Solomon asked for the gift that keeps on giving: wisdom. He realized that the greatness of a king was not in his wealth and power, but in his ability to rule fairly and justly over the people. His request was that he would be given the discernment and understanding necessary to do just that.

Solomon's request for wisdom was the equivalent of being given one wish by a genie and asking for unlimited wishes. The Lord responded favorably to Solomon's request and the outcome was remarkable.

The Lord was pleased that Solomon had asked for this. So God said to him, "Since you have asked for this and not for long life or wealth for yourself, nor have asked for the death of your enemies but for discernment in administering justice, I will do what you have asked. I will give you a wise and discerning heart, so that there will never have been anyone like you, nor will there ever be. Moreover, I will give you what you have not asked for—both wealth and honor—so that in your lifetime you will have no equal among kings." (1 Kings 3:10-13)

Wisdom, like grace, is something the Lord loves to lavish upon his people. He will never withhold it and desperately wants his people to attain it, because wisdom gives us the ability to navigate our spiritually defective DNA and a broken world. Wisdom, when applied, produces holiness in our lives and communities and allows us to live in a way that points people toward Jesus.

In his desire for generations after him to have the wisdom and understanding he had attained, Solomon passed on a precious book of the Bible, Proverbs, as a gift to his descendants. However, as you'll recall from the story of Solomon's son, Rehoboam, who ascended to the throne after his father, wisdom can be shared, but it is only experienced when it is applied. Many of us have had the experience of hearing the wisdom of our parents and ignoring it. That often leads to a failure that could have been avoided. What happened to Rehoboam could happen to any of us. It is completely possible to know wisdom but not be wise.

Wise people apply their knowledge and understanding to make decisions that are good for themselves and others, as well as honoring to God. When we act wisely, we allow ourselves and others to flourish. Wisdom leads to love, justice, fairness, and holiness, and it helps us understand the heart of God.

When I was thirteen years old I stepped into the greatest failure of my life. I knew what the right decision was, but I ignored it out of a desire to have an experience I thought I needed. I spiraled into a tunnel of guilt, shame, and depression. Afterward I shared what had happened with my father. Instead of bringing down a punishment, he gave me a Bible and shared with me the book of Proverbs. He understood that my punishment was the emotional anguish I was experiencing, and that the knowledge of the hurt my decision brought upon others was something I was going to have to live with my entire life. In his love and desire for me to not experience that degree of pain again, he pointed me to wisdom. He knew I would need it to navigate my teenage years and come out on the other side a mature young man who didn't make the same foolish decisions as my friends.

Proverbs has thirty-one chapters, and many months have thirty-one days. I embraced a month-long journey of meditating on one chapter per day. I was determined to learn wisdom and apply it to avoid another incident like the one I had just walked through. Of course it didn't work one hundred percent of the time, and I still made some unwise decisions. However, that foundation of wisdom has helped me avoid many pains, heartaches, and failures. Wisdom has led to decisions that brought life and holiness into the world rather than death, destruction, and pain.

As a young leader it is to your benefit to meditate on the wisdom literature of the Bible. The Scripture you spend time with now will be with you throughout your entire life. Wisdom will protect your heart, inform your mind, and give you perspective and mental strength. Wisdom leads to decisions that bring about life and restoration.

When we exercise wisdom it brings about great joy in the heart of God. James 1:5 says, "If any of you lacks wisdom, you should ask God, who gives generously to all without finding fault, and it will be given to you." Just as my father gave me the book of Proverbs in my time of need, so God gives these books to us all so that we might know his heart and hear his voice in all that we do.

How are you becoming a lover of wisdom? When you look at your life do you see times when you knew what was right, but chose what was wrong? What can you do to ensure that your future experiences will be different? In what ways does God want to grow your mind and heart so that you might better love him and those around you?

PEOPLE WILL ALWAYS BE PEOPLE

A guy in my middle school guys small groups once asked me, "What's the best part of being a Christian leader?" My answer was simple: "The people." He followed up with another question. "What is the hardest part of being a Christian leader?" My answer was the same: "The people." He laughed, and so did I. I love people—but they are difficult. The church is full of imperfect people, including ourselves. We will make mistakes and hurt others, and they will do the same to us. Just because we are followers of Jesus doesn't mean we're incapable of causing deep hurt.

Throughout Scripture are stories of people who do amazing faith-filled things for God, and stories of those exact same people making awful decisions that bring about great pain and brokenness. Peter declares he will follow Jesus to the cross, and that same night he denies Jesus three times. David declares an unfailing, steadfast love for God's laws and commands, then commits murder and adultery. Sarah, Abraham's wife, is faithful to God, but banishes her stepson to die in the desert.

Faith-filled, Jesus-loving, God-honoring people will do both good and evil. As the apostle Paul puts it in Romans 7:15, "I do not understand what I do. For what I want to do I do not do, but what I hate I do." This is the internal struggle of the human heart.

The good news is that God's love is unfailing and unchanging, despite the fragile and fickle hearts of people. As it says in Hebrews 13:8, "Jesus Christ is the same yesterday and today and forever." The grace, favor, and friendship of Jesus are unchanging, and they give us courage and freedom to love, forgive, and serve even the people who have hurt us the most.

In your lifetime you will be in relationships with hundreds, if not thousands, of people. Together you will laugh, cry, dream, celebrate, and share moments of your lives. With these people you will experience beauty, and you will also experience darkness and human weakness. The only thing that will keep your heart healthy in these times is your relationship with Jesus. How often have you let him down? How often have you betrayed him? How often does your flesh keep you from doing what the Spirit is calling you to? For me it is daily. Yet I rest in one truth. Despite myself, he loves me, and continues to pursue friendship with me. As a young leader there are times when you will be hurt, outcast, frustrated, or disappointed by other people. In those moments push into the grace you have received from Jesus, and become a mature leader who continually extends grace to others.

Reflection Questions: Going Forward

1. The chapter begins with how Dan hears from God. What are ways you personally hear from him?

2. What can we do as a student leadership team to listen more to God?

3. Come up with some examples of faith-stretching or risk-taking goals for your leadership team or youth group. Examples could be that each member of the leadership team, between now and the next meeting, would have at least one conversation with a peer about faith, or that four new people would come to youth group next Wednesday, or that someone would actually come to faith in Jesus at the winter retreat.

4. This chapter described how we as leaders must also be learners. Name a couple of the most important things you have learned through this book and your student leadership team's meetings.

5. Close this gathering with prayers of gratitude to the Lord for what we've learned from this book, for each other, and for the bright future we have in front of us as a group.

CONTINUAL TRANSFORMATION

Good leaders are always growing and changing. Who you are today is different from who you will be in ten years. As you follow Jesus and maintain a close friendship with him, he will continue to shape you into the person you were always meant to be. Years from today you will wake up and realize you are different than you were before, and better spiritually than you have been.

Bill Gates, the founder of Microsoft, is known for this quote: "We always overestimate the change that will occur in the next two years and underestimate the change that will occur in the next ten."[11] Leadership growth, spiritual and emotional maturity, and a strong sense of identity are not things that form in days, but in decades. While you may wish to already be fully transformed, Jesus doesn't expect that. He wants to journey with you your whole life, and he will be there your whole life to help you become the person he intends you to be.

He will speak into your life when you are ready to listen. He will lead you into experiences that will shape your heart, mind, and soul when he knows you are ready. He will redeem the horrible things that happen to you, and the messes you create. He will be there for not only the highlights of your life, but the most mundane days. He will see it all and be in it all, and no matter what you do, whatever happens to you, or where you go, he will always be pleased to call you a friend.

End Notes

1. Central Intelligence Agency, "Infant Mortality Rate," *The World Factbook, Central Intelligence Agency:* https://www.cia.gov/library/publications/the-world-factbook/fields/2091.html.

2. R. A. Torrey, *How to Pray* (Old Tappan, New Jersey: Fleming H. Revell Company. 5th ed., 1975).

3. Spiritually Defective DNA, a phrase used with permission from Tom Lundeen, senior pastor at Riverside Church of Big Lake, Minnesota.

4. Martin Luther King Jr. "I Have a Dream." Speech presented at the March on Washington for Jobs and Freedom, Washington, D.C., August 1968. http://avalon.law.yale.edu/20th_century/mlk01.asp.

5. National Hockey League, "Wayne Gretzky," *Players, National Hockey League:* www.nhl.com/player/wayne-gretzky-8447400.

6. Rob Reiner, dir. *A Few Good Men.* Columbia Pictures, 1992, DVD.

7. Barna Group, "Americans Divided on the Importance of Church," *Barna,* https://www.barna.com/research/americans-divided-on-the-importance-of-church-/#.V-hxhlVy6FD.

8. Pew Research Center, "America's Changing Religious Landscape," *Pew Research Center,* http://www.pewforum.org/2015/05/12/americas-changing-religious-landscape.

9. Shel Silverstein, *The Giving Tree* (New York: Harper & Row, 1964).

10. Ernest Hemingway, *Across the River and Into the Trees* (London: Johnathan Cape Ltd., 1952).

11. Bill Gates, Nathan Myhrvold, and Peter Rinearson, *The Road Ahead* (New York: Viking, 1995).